The Theory and Practice of Multicultural Education

The Theory and Practice of Multicultural Education

A Focus on the K–12 Educational Setting

Chinaka S. DomNwachukwu

ROWMAN & LITTLEFIELD
Lanham • Boulder • New York • London

Published by Rowman & Littlefield
A wholly owned subsidiary of The Rowman & Littlefield Publishing Group, Inc.
4501 Forbes Boulevard, Suite 200, Lanham, Maryland 20706
www.rowman.com

Unit A, Whitacre Mews, 26-34 Stannary Street, London SE11 4AB

Copyright © 2018 by Chinaka S. DomNwachukwu

All rights reserved. No part of this book may be reproduced in any form or by any electronic or mechanical means, including information storage and retrieval systems, without written permission from the publisher, except by a reviewer who may quote passages in a review.

British Library Cataloguing in Publication Information Available

Library of Congress Cataloging-in-Publication Data Available

ISBN: 978-1-4758-3729-2 (cloth : alk. paper)
ISBN: 978-1-4758-3730-8 (pbk. : alk. paper)
ISBN: 978-1-4758-3731-5 (electronic)

∞™ The paper used in this publication meets the minimum requirements of American National Standard for Information Sciences—Permanence of Paper for Printed Library Materials, ANSI/NISO Z39.48-1992.

Printed in the United States of America

Contents

List of Figures vii

Acknowledgments ix

Introduction xi

1   The Learner and the Educational Process   1

2   Humans as Cultural Beings: Foundations for Multicultural Education   13

3   Engaging the American Cultural Mosaic   31

4   Engaging the Crises of Cross-Cultural Encounters   57

5   Educational Inequalities in the American Schools   83

6   Historical Foundations of Multicultural Education in the United States   95

7   Standards-Based Planning and Teaching in a Multicultural Classroom   113

Notes 133

References 143

Index 153

About the Author 159

List of Figures

Figure 2.1.	Defining the Human Person	15
Figure 2.2.	The Scientific View of Humans	16
Figure 3.1.	Charles Kraft's Cultural Patterns	38
Figure 3.2.	American Cultural Patterning	39
Figure 3.3.	Interactions of Cultural Structures in the American Cultural Systems	45
Figure 3.4.	Worldview in Cultural Arrangements	47
Figure 3.5.	Worldview Alterations	53
Figure 4.1.	Issues in Discrimination	58
Figure 4.2.	Development of Cross-Cultural Ideas	69
Figure 7.1.	Framework for Twenty-First-Century Learning	114

Acknowledgments

This book is possible because of the opportunity granted to me by my employer, Azusa Pacific University, to take a sabbatical and engage in research for this book. For that I am very grateful. I am also grateful for the support given to me by the dean of the School of Education, Anita Henck. Alan Jones, editor of *Multicultural Education* magazine, and the executive secretary of the California Council on Teacher Education, has continued to be a reliable support system. As I was about to begin the sabbatical, I contacted him and solicited his input on what he considered current issues in multicultural education. Not only did he provide helpful insights, he was willing to read through my manuscript and offer feedback. Sherwood Thomson, professor at Eastern Kentucky University, invested his personal time to read through my manuscript and furnished very helpful observations. Kimberly Battle-Waters Denu, vice president and chief diversity officer at Azusa Pacific University, willingly read through my manuscript and provided useful feedback. JoAnn Jurchan, a faculty colleague, also read through one of the chapters on the practice of multicultural education and provided good feedback as well.

I am eternally grateful to my wife, Nkechi, whose enduring support and constant critique helps to keep me on my toes. She tolerated my spending my entire sabbatical on this project because I was working on a deadline. My children Osinachi, Chinonso, Naedum, and Nissi remain my strength and motivation as their love and support make me look forward to each day with joyous expectations. Finally, I am indebted to God the father of our Lord Jesus Christ, the source of my knowledge and strength, the sustainer of my life, who has upheld me through this work amid the many other demands on my time and attention.

Introduction

This book is the first of three books in a series, which are replacing my first book on this topic, *An Introduction to Multicultural Education: From Theory to Practice*. I began this project with the goal of revising the original book, but along the way, through a conversation between myself and the publishers, we decided to split the materials into three separate books.

This first book in the collection sets the stage for the conversation about multicultural education in the United States, with implications and applications that have direct relevance beyond the American shores. This volume attempts to provide foundational principles, theories, and practices that should undergird multicultural education in American schools and beyond. It presents these principles, theories, and practices in language that is comprehensible to the average beginning-level educator.

The book targets educators at various levels of the profession: beginning, developing, and accomplished. It is written for the higher education institutions, educational organizations, and practitioners who prepare K–12 educators for the K–12 educational setting. It's a book every student of cultural diversity and multicultural education must read.

The book begins by placing the theory and practice of multicultural education in the United States within a historical context. It traces the historical foundations of multicultural education far into the early days of American colonies, engaged education in the post–Civil War era through the Jim Crow era, the civil rights period, and into the twenty-first century. It discusses the impacts of the civil rights movement, government legislations, and the contributions of educators to the history and development of multicultural education.

The subsequent chapters articulate an understanding of the role of education in the larger society and its implications in the shaping of an informed populace. An in-depth discussion of the topics of culture, cultural competency, cross-cultural encounters and interactions, and their implications for our global society are addressed. The challenge of educational inequalities in America's schools is confronted, and practical methods for implementing multicultural education are presented.

Recognizing the unique character of our twenty-first-century world as a global village, this book, written by an African-born and U.S.-based educator, presents a perspective to which educators all over the world should pay special attention.

Chapter One

The Learner and the Educational Process

> **Chapter Objectives:**
>
> This chapter introduces multicultural education as learner-centered pedagogy. It defines education, what it means to learn and to teach, and who a learner is. Readers will be able to do the following:
>
> 1. Articulate an understanding of the role of education in the larger society
> 2. Define a learner, a teacher, and what it means to learn within the larger educational setting

The twenty-first-century teaching and learning context has seen a growing demand for purposeful implementation of learner-centered pedagogical practices. Moate and Cox (2015) described learner-centered pedagogy as nonlinear and multidimensional learning activities that occur within a social context.[1] The term pedagogy has often been used to mean the art or profession of teaching or instruction.[2] While some in the academy have often used pedagogy to refer to teaching in general, it is actually a misuse of the term. Pedagogy, in its historic and practical meanings, refers to the art or science of teaching children.[3]

The word *pedagogy* derives from a Greek root of *paidagogia* or *pedagogos*. This refers to a slave whose job was to take children to and from the school where they received instruction.[4] The distinguishing marks of pedagogy, which include a setting where the teacher decides, plans, and directs what and how students learn, are not fit for the adult population. In pedagogy, it is assumed that the learner needs to depend on the teacher for both motivation to learn and for selection, planning, and delivery of learning material. This means that the teacher, not the student, is at the center of the learning engagement. This is different from *andragogy*.

The evolution of the term andragogy is traced back to 1833 when a German educationist by the name of Alexander Kapp coined the word. The term has continued to be used and extended until today when it has taken on a new life and meaning within academia.[5] Andragogy has been defined by some as learner-centered education. If that's the case, it means that andragogy may not be focused on adult learners alone but on all who learn in a learner-centered context, whether children or adults. In his protest against the traditional authoritative education of the past, John Dewey called for a learner-focused education, where the learner takes the central place in the educational process.

While some have seen elements of andragogy in Dewey's progressive education,[6] it is important to see more of a constructivist focus in Dewey than andragogy, because Dewey's focus was on the lab school, where children engaged with the learning experience by doing things with their hands.[7] In 1980, Malcom Knowles extended the meaning of andragogy by identifying six main assumptions of andragogy, which have direct relevance to adult learning modalities:

- Self-Concept—This assumes that the adult learner is an autonomous, self-directed, and independent learner, who would resist situations in which they feel that someone else is imposing their will upon them.
- The Role of Experience—Adult learners come to the learning context with a repository of experiences from which they can draw to enrich their learning, unlike children who don't have that.
- Readiness to Learn—Adults are considered ready to learn once they have determined that they need the learning experience. This means that they don't need an extrinsic motivation to learn, rather their desire to learn is motivated from within.
- Orientation to Learning—Adults tend to learn for the purpose of putting into use what they learned in the immediate context, unlike children who learn for the future. This means that adult learners would be motivated to learn to the extent that they see the learning experience as useful in solving real-life problems.
- Internal Motivation—Adults may feel pressure from the outside to learn, but they respond better to internal motivation to learn rather than external motivation.
- The Need to Know—Adult learners engage because they know the value of the learning experience, and they are willing to invest the required time, money, and resources to attain that knowledge.[8]

Heutagogy, on the other hand, has emerged as a step above andragogy in the adult learning experience. *Heutagogy* is defined as the principle of self-determined learning and a natural progression from the previous "-gogies" (pedagogy and andragogy). According to Kenyon and Hase (2001), heutagogy provides the optimal way to approach learning in the twenty-first century. It is said to reflect the way the world of learning has changed and recognizes the multiple skills and competencies needed for the twenty-first-century workplace.[9]

Heutagogy, according to Ashton and Newman (2006), looks to a future that sees how to learn as a fundamental educational skill. Kenyon and Hase (2001) see heutagogy as one step above andragogy. In heutagogy you have learners who are able to read across critical issues, to question issues, and to determine what is of interest or relevance to them. Learners can negotiate their learning experiences to meet their set goals and objectives. It affirms a learning environment characterized by flexibility, in which the teacher provides learning resources, but the learner designs the learning experience by negotiating around his or her self-determined needs.[10]

The twenty-first-century educational setting requires that the teacher understands the learner in a unique way: the learner's age, culture, language, academic skills and abilities, and the social environment of the teaching and learning, as well as the curriculum. These are a prerequisite knowledge base for effective learner-based pedagogical practices.

A learner-centered pedagogy, therefore, requires that we understand the meaning of education, define teaching and learning, and be able to fully grasp the nature of the interaction that takes place between the teacher, the learner, and the content and context of learning. It is the objective of this chapter to establish that the nature of this interaction makes multicultural education an inescapable reality in the American educational settings.

WHAT IS EDUCATION?

Education has been defined as the process of training and developing the mind and character of a person. It is the process of imparting knowledge and skill through formal schooling, teaching, or training.[11] Education as a process has often been defined as the inculcation of knowledge. This definition first presupposes a source of knowledge; secondly, it presupposes a substance or material called knowledge, and lastly a receptor. The source is often called the teacher in the formal educational setting; the substance is often called information, ideas, or instructional content; and the receptor is the learner.

The definition above introduces a number of issues in education, namely, training, knowledge development, impartation of skills, development of the mind and character, issues around formal schooling, and finally, the art or science of teaching. The concept of knowledge development suggests a process of cultivating, planting, and nurturing knowledge as part of the educational process. This makes the teacher-versus-learner relationship indispensable in the educational process. It also suggests that education is both a matter of the "mind" as well as the "hand" when it talks about skills acquisition and the mind as a faculty undergoing development.

The formal schooling process is generally considered necessary for meaningful education to take place. One essential ingredient that makes for a schooling system is the teacher-to-learner relationship. This relationship does not take place in a cultural vacuum. The teacher approaches teaching through his or her personal cultural lenses, while the student approaches learning through his or her own cultural lenses.

When teachers are unable to connect with students and their cultural backgrounds, or students are unable to connect with teachers because of cultural differences, the educational process is shortchanged. This understanding of education suggests that it is a social contract, not necessarily an intellectual contract, as may seem to be the case in B. F. Skinner's definition of education as "the culture of the intellect."[12]

Skinner's definition means that education is something that happens within the realm of the intellect or the mind. His definition may stand critical inquiry if we can look at education as a process of the mind, and skills acquisition as the end product of the educational process, or its fruit. It simply means that skills acquisition may be part of the educational process, but the practical application or use of the acquired skills is not education, instead it is called production.

With due respect to his vast contributions to clinical psychology, education, behavioral medicine, brain study, and mental retardation,[13] and without in any way minimizing Skinner's contribution to the educational process, his definition of education as the culture of the intellect, nevertheless, does not explain the whole educational process, and compels us to look at Plato's allegory of the cave for further clarification on the nature of education.

The allegory of the cave illustrates the meaning of education in a nutshell. Plato talked about prisoners in an underground cave who were chained down so they could not move around. They saw the real world only in the form of reflections cast against the wall of the cave by burning fires. These images appear in disfigured and irregular forms so much that the images have no semblance to the realities out there.

The prisoners get used to these images and are convinced that the images are realities in themselves. They have no knowledge of the realities out there so they hold on to their half-baked knowledge of reality as the one and only truth about reality. To convince them otherwise, Plato suggests unchaining them and taking them out to the world of reality. This allegory has a lot of implications for understanding the educational process.

Education is an enculturation process. The learner shares a lot of commonalities with Plato's prisoners. They are limited in their knowledge and ideas about the world of reality, and the educational process is supposed to unlock learners from that prison and release them into the world of reality.

Education is supposed to be an empowering process, which transforms one from the world of ignorance to knowledge. It's the process by which the prisoners are persuaded to engage the realities outside of the cave and to confront the fact of the flaws of their perception. This is done either by unchaining them and taking them outside of the cave to confront reality face-to-face, or by attempting to persuade them by mere word of mouth to begin to look at reality differently. Looking at it from a contemporary perspective, you can also describe it as flooding their minds and perceptions with new ideas of reality.

If the goal is to release the prisoners from the perceptual blindness created by their confinement, the ideal would be to release them from the chains and take them outside the cave. But if the goal is to create doubts in their minds that they have a full grasp of reality, or at least to provoke their thoughts to consider such a possibility, mere information may as well do it. It certainly takes one who has earned the trust and confidence of the prisoner to unchain him and persuade him to step outside of his phantom world to the world of reality.

Based on this interpretation of the allegory of the cave, one must question a definition of education that sees it exclusively as the transmission of information, as to whether it is fully representative of the meaning of education. The goal of education has to be to produce new and altered human persons significantly different from who they were before entering the educational process. This aims at both social, intellectual, and skills transformation. The educated person must emerge a new and better person than he or she was before entering the educational process. For this reason, information transmission alone does not do it; a restructuring and reorientation of the total person takes place in the educational process.

The educational context becomes, therefore, the best place to create and construct socially informed and civically responsible citizens. One of the fundamental flaws that developed in the United States education system, which was not challenged until recently, has been the impartation of knowledge with no attempt to develop socially informed citizens who are committed to harmonious and respectful social coexistence in a diverse society like the United States.

Most U.S. children come to school ignorant of the world around them and ignorant of the many different peoples that populate their communities. We educate them in the imprisonment of their minds and in small homogeneous communities and fail to expose them to the mosaic world of reality that makes America what it is. These students, whether raised in the white suburban communities of Iowa, or in the African-American communities of Harlem and South-Central Los Angeles, the world they know is, exclusively, their own cultural world.

The world outside of the communities from which these children come are alien to them, and the educational settings work hard to keep it so, rather than unchain them from such imprisonments, to expose them to the discomforting, yet necessary, world of reality beyond their comfort zones. This is a fundamental flaw with the U.S. educational system, which must be confronted for America to produce global citizens, not just the ethnocentric bigots that fill many American institutions. This is the place and purpose of multicultural education in the American educational system.

WHAT DOES IT MEAN TO TEACH?

It must be underscored here that the transmission or presentation of information is not synonymous to teaching. To teach involves a series of more complex processes, which are encountered in the everyday attempt to both influence students and transmit knowledge. The information being transmitted during a process of communication is one entity, the communicator is another entity, and the recipient of the information is another.

The communicator must first understand and appropriate the information to the extent that he or she feels competent and comfortable enough to communicate it to another person with the intention of effecting some changes in the life or thinking of the recipient, which is the learner. Many teachers transmit information they themselves have not grasped, internalized, or fully apprehended, and yet they claim to be teachers.

An individual may take in a coded message without understanding what it means and can relay the same message to another person without additions or distortions. That would not be teaching. Teaching, which imparts knowledge, must effect a change in personality and perspective in both the teacher and the student.

The allegory of the cave, once again, presents a classic case of what it means to teach. The teacher is like the first prisoner to be released from the chain. The first prisoner who is released and exposed to the world of reality faces the challenge of returning to the cave and convincing his other friends that there is more to reality than they were beholding. For him to do that effectively he must not be reciting previously memorized texts, but must speak about personal encounters and personal transformation.

It takes a culturally and socially transformed teacher to impart a life-transforming and culturally sensitive education. The prisoner must be persuasive enough to get other prisoners to take him seriously, to get them to begin to give some credibility to his ideas and thoughts. Such a development would only arise if there are physically convincing proofs that the teacher can employ to make his or her point. This introduces the idea of methodology. Possessing the information alone does not make for a good teacher, but possessing the right method for communicating his or her information and effecting changes in lives makes a difference. Educators call these strategies.

In effect, therefore, to teach means both to model and to instruct with effective strategies. The teacher must be standing at the point where he or she wants to bring the students before attempting to get them to come on to that level of enlightenment. According to B. F. Skinner, the teacher instructs, informs, forms, and shapes the student. Teaching is the expediting of the learning process. Skinner cautions that the teacher does not transmit his own behaviors to the student; instead he imparts knowledge that may include meanings, concepts, facts, and propositions.[14]

One must part way with Skinner here to state that it is practically impossible for the teacher to avoid imparting his behaviors onto his students. Effective teachers do not just impart information, they impart themselves.

The art of teaching is not just the transmission of information. Skinner had said to teach means to "help the student learn," "nourish or cultivate" the child.[15] The term cultivate, an agricultural term, presupposes planting and tending with the expectation of blossom and fruitfulness. To cultivate is to invest time and effort with an eager expectation for proceeds. Teaching as cultivation involves the investment of time and energy by the teacher into the student with the hope and expectation that the student will blossom and produce fruits that justify the energy that has been poured on her.

A question every multicultural educator must ask him- or herself is this: "What kind of students do I want to produce?" You are planting and cultivating students who will unavoidably grow up to represent your ideas, worldviews, and even your principles. You will often be remembered and quoted long after they have left you. How would you want to be remembered, represented, and quoted?

We must concede to Skinner, to an extent, that teaching is not an attempt on the side of the teacher to reproduce himself, rather it involves the task of helping the learner discover how to fully actualize him- or herself. To teach is to bring the learner to the point at which he or she can begin to ask the right questions, the questions whose answers alone can place that learner on the road to self-realization and self-actualization.

WHAT DOES IT MEAN TO LEARN?

A major point B. F. Skinner makes about learning is that it can take place with or without the teacher, but that the degree of learning varies in each given situation. To learn is seen by Skinner as to acquire or receive education. He uses such verbs as *grasp*, *impress*, *drill*, and *inculcate* to describe what happens when concepts and ideas are transferred from the teacher to the student.

To learn, therefore, would mean to "absorb," as in soaking up something; "digest," as in chewing and swallowing; "conceive," as in impregnation by accepting from someone else the seminal fluid and conceiving of a child; or "contract," as in the medical process of getting an infection.[16]

Skinner's ideas suggest the transference of some concrete substance from the teacher to the learner. Once the learner accepts the substance it becomes his or her own possession, no longer the teacher's. Learning, however, goes beyond these ideas of Skinner. It is a process by which one's exposure to concepts and ideas in the educational context brings one to the point of both reflection and meditation.

Education takes an individual beyond that point to discover what he is capable of being if he can rightly and adequately apply and utilize the resources around him. Abstract learning has no place in this definition of learning. Any learning that ends with the acquisition of ideas and concepts that are irrelevant to practical living and existence does not constitute full learning; instead while it may stretch and challenge the mind, it may constitute a waste of time and life resources if it has no utilitarian purpose.

To learn, therefore, is to accept modifications, intellectual or otherwise, which would bring one's life into contact with more enriching experiences and opportunities in the real life. It is to accept to change one's perspective or direction for the better. To learn is to grow richer and taller in the quality of life as well as in intellectual capacity. Through education, therefore, we construct individuals and consequently a society. Therefore, multicultural education must take a central place in our educational practices.

We not only impart knowledge in the classrooms, we construct individuals and social arrangements. Appreciation, respect, equality, and mutual coexistence, which are central to multicultural education, must be consciously constructed in the classrooms.

A learner, therefore, is one who is on a journey. The individual is on a journey to self-realization and self-actualization. A learner opens the self to the intrusion of new and foreign ideas and concepts, with the hope that in sieving through them he or she would have access to some knowledge, ideas, rules, and/or resources that would increase the quality of his or her own life.

A learner is not only motivated by the teacher and his presentation of the subject matter, but also by his or her own dreams and aspirations. He has clear goals and expectations along with the goals and expectations that the teacher has set, and the ones that are inherent in the subject of study. These internal goals develop over time. Learning, therefore, must be seen as a lifelong undertaking. The journey may begin early in one's childhood, but does not (or should not) end until one is dead.

If humanity is such a complex entity as we have described in this work, and if teaching and learning are such intricate undertakings, what then is possible in the classroom? Abraham Maslow saw human development in a unique way. According to him, the age of sixty and above is the age of self-actualization. According to Maslow, at the stage of self-actualization, the individual begins to live out one's real self. At this stage, the individual begins to work to fulfill his life mission and personal potential, and to conduct the self with characters that reflect full maturity.[17]

If Maslow was right that the self-actualizing age is sixty plus, it means that most people in the classroom are on a journey.[18] Since many teachers retire by age sixty, it means the bulk of the teachers in the classrooms are still seeking. They are learners along with their students, on a journey to self-discovery and self-actualization. This gives reasons to accept the view that the classroom is "an experiment in human possibilities."[19] This points to the possibilities of what a teacher can become as well as the students. How many teachers are open to these possibilities? Sadly there are not very many.

The young adult teacher is asking questions like "Where am I going from here?" "What else does life have for me apart from what I can see right now?" The senior adult is asking, "Is this all there is to life?" "Is there life after retirement?" The younger students are asking, "What does the future hold for me?" "Will I be a success or a failure?" The classroom nevertheless holds possibilities for each of these individuals; in it they can see their own power to help and shape tomorrow for themselves and others.

The hope, therefore, is that the teacher can find, within the classroom walls, answers to the questions of both the teacher and the students. The teacher will then be more likely to work harder to become the best teacher he or she can be, since success in what the teacher is doing right now will very much impact his or her sense of validation as a human being or of frustration and worthlessness in the long run. One teacher may take the challenge and become the best teacher ever, while another may surrender to the worthlessness and futility of life and refuse to attempt to make much out of life. The teacher could say, "If all there is to life is work, live, and die, why bother?"

Students as well may see the classroom as the context in which they can take charge of their lives and launch out into a mission of self-actualization and apply themselves to change the world. These students will likely apply themselves through discipline and hard work, whereas others may see only their lack of opportunities and possibilities, and for that reason refuse to do anything to launch ahead.

The classroom presents us with a laboratory for viewing the fullest extent of human potential as well as the lowest depth of human failure. The variables that exist in each situation are the ways each individual perceives who they are and examines their chances for successes and failures.

One would wish that every teacher sees the classroom as the context where he or she must fully explore and utilize personal strengths and potentials, become a super teacher if there is any such thing, and if it is attainable. One must learn patience for the weak, become a vehicle that must transmit respect, tolerance, life, and hope to all students. As a teacher, you must desire that your students become successful and self-actualized citizens, as you strive to become a successful and self-actualized citizen yourself.

In conclusion, the point must be made that contrary to many predictions of the 1990s, the teacher has not yet been replaced by computers, and it doesn't look they will be replaced soon. Even the computers need the teacher to teach them what to teach.

QUESTIONS AND APPLICATION

Case Study: Dealing with Stereotypes

Background

You are a Chinese female teacher in a predominantly Hispanic neighborhood school. This is your first teaching assignment. During teacher preparation program you developed a special passion for the inner-city schools. You wanted to work in these challenging neighborhoods to make a difference in the lives of students who rarely get the best of teachers and resources. You had an offer to work in a reputable suburban district, but you turned it down for this inner-city school job. You were looking forward to this new experience of doing something that would positively impact young lives.

The Problem

Your first week in the new school has been a major shock. The first day your car was broken into and valuables worth more than $800.00 were removed. On the second day upon arrival at school you entered your classroom and were shocked to see all kinds of graffiti written on the walls. There were some writings in plain English that stated, "This place is not for dog eaters." On the third day, one student raised his hand to ask a question, when you called on him, instead of addressing the lesson of the hour, his question was "how does dog meat taste?" This led to an outburst of laughter in the classroom. At this point you are beginning to see a connection between the vandalism on your car, the graffiti, and the racial slur that you are now facing.

CHALLENGE

a. How would you feel as a result of these encounters?
b. What response, if any, would you give to the student who asked the question?
c. Would you address the whole class on this subject? Why? Why not?
d. What would you say to them if you choose to address them on the topic?
e. What steps would you take to ensure that your life, property, and self-esteem are protected in this new environment?
f. What short- or long-term decision would you make concerning your decision to teach in the inner-city schools?
g. Would you involve the school administration in this matter? If yes, how and why?

REVIEW QUESTIONS

a. What is education? In view of the insights gained from this chapter, articulate your understanding of the purpose of education within the larger society.
b. As one who sees teaching as your vocation, articulate a personal mission statement that outlines how you see your role as a teacher in the K–12 classrooms.
c. Define your role as a learner within the classroom setting, who also happens to be
d. a teacher at the same time.

STRATEGIES FOR APPLICATION IN THE K–12 CLASSROOMS

1. *Grades K–12*: Teach your students to memorize the following chant and recite it to themselves and to the class.

> *I am a human being. I have a future.*
> *It's my honor as a Student to do my best.*
> *It's my honor as a Scholar to do my best.*

As a follow-up activity discuss the benefits of performing well at school and the impact it can have on their quality of life into the future. Discuss those lucrative jobs and activities such as being a renowned musician, actor/actress, and athlete. Discuss the demographic representation of this population compared to the larger U.S. population and make clear that the chances of becoming one of these rich individuals may not be very high for everyone, making schooling the next best way to advance one's self.

2. *Grades 4–12*: Ask your students to project how much money they want to make each year to be able to live at the comfort level they desire. Secure U.S. census data on income distribution across professions, showing earning for college-educated individuals and non-college-educated individuals. Lead them to use the chart you have provided to determine how many years of schooling they need to afford the quality of life they desire.

Chapter Two

Humans as Cultural Beings
Foundations for Multicultural Education

Chapter Objectives:

The purpose of this chapter is to expose readers to the concept of culture and cultural identity using personal narratives, rather than abstract concepts and lectures on culture and worldview. After completing this chapter, readers will be able to do the following:

1. Articulate an understanding of multicultural education as a learner-centered pedagogy
2. Critique the concept of culture from their personal experiences
3. Based on the insights from this chapter and their personal experiences, they will articulate a cultural autobiography
4. Develop a personal appreciation of cultural diversity by explaining why it is an asset, not a liability within the field of education

---

This chapter anchors on what scholars have identified as cultural identity theory. Cultural identity theory focuses on the assumption that humans use various communicative processes to negotiate and construct their cultural identities and relationships within given contexts. The concept has been adopted in relation to group identities such as nationality, race, ethnicity, age, sex, sexuality, gender, socioeconomic status, regional identities, ethnolinguistic identities, political affiliations, and disabilities.[1] To engage the quest for understanding humans as cultural beings, this study must first attempt to understand humans as beings, and then engage them within the context of culture.

The teaching and learning of diversity and diversity issues anchors on people—teachers and students. One of the most positive experiences of this author as a teacher of social equity and justice as well as multiculturalism has been the process of helping my students come to terms with their cultural identity. Many native-born Caucasian Americans (commonly called "whites," a term that does not fit an adequate description of the pigmentation of any human group) assume that beyond being white and being American, there are no more cultural constructs that would distinguish them from other people within the American society. When these individuals are persuaded (as is often the case) to dig deeper into their cultural roots, they discover, to their amazement, that Caucasian or white could be Anglo, Dutch, Greek, Russian, Jewish, Arab, Iranian, and many more. It is not a valid cultural identity.

The reality of multicultural education, however, is that it takes one who knows who he or she is within a cultural setting to enhance other people's cultural awareness and promote diversity, thus the question, "who am I within my culture?" Identity negotiation is a critical aspect of the intercultural experience, and teachers who work in multicultural settings go through this negotiation just like their students do.

In this chapter, we will examine some ways individuals within the American educational systems have attempted to describe their cultural identity. Before articulating individual understanding of cultural identity, we need to discuss what it means to be human within the context of multicultural education.

WHAT DOES IT MEAN TO BE HUMAN?

The quest for the definition of what it means to be human has been the preoccupation of philosophers and scientists from the time of Socrates until today. We are generally regarded by scientists and anthropologists as *Homo sapiens,* or human individuals. Physical anthropology has reduced the definition of "human" to two categories of biology and culture in which the two elements that distinguish humans from other animals are certain unique biological traits such as intellect as well as the human ability to develop and maintain culture (Nelson and Jurmain 1985).

Some theorists have attempted to define us based on our self-consciousness or what we call the ego. Norman Ford (1988) made a definitive statement that humans are social beings by nature. According to him, awareness of the self or personal ego is only possible because of man's conscious activities. These activities can be corporeal or non-corporeal. Among the different forms in which this sense of self is manifested is cultural and social activities.[2]

Humans as Cultural Beings

Harold H. Titus in his *Living Issues in Philosophy* (1970, 1995) gave a definition that encapsulates what it means to be human much better than any other sources consulted on this topic. He defined the human being as a part of nature who partakes in nature's ways, yet appears to transcend nature and exercises control over it.[3] He writes about the human being,[4]

> [H]e is no less than what he is—a self-conscious being with unique characteristics. The nature and character of a thing is determined not so much by its beginning as by its end. Man's aspirations give him his place and his importance. . . . He also has great adaptive powers and the capacity to exert some control over his own development.

Titus presents three perspectives from which we can look at the human person, namely, (1) the classical view of man, the rationalistic view of man; (2) the religious view of man; and (3) the scientific interpretation of man.

The classical Greek view is built around the thoughts of great philosophers like Plato, Aristotle, and Protagoras. Whereas Plato thinks that reason is the

Figure 2.1. Defining the Human Person

highest part of the human soul, whose function is to guide conduct, Aristotle sees reason as man's prized faculty, which sets him apart from subhuman nature. This classical interpretation sees humans primarily from the viewpoint of nature and our unique rational abilities. This view can be stretched to its humanistic conclusion in which Protagoras suggests that man is the measure of all things (Jarrett 1969).

The religious view—which according to Titus (1970) is represented by Judeo-Christian, Islamic, and Hindu traditions—looks at humans from a spiritual pair of lenses. The Judeo-Christian perspective looks at human beings primarily from the point of view of their divine origin. Humans transcend the natural conditions and reach their highest potential when in harmony with God. Islam sees man's duty as loyalty to God and his divine laws, and that is the essence of his being. Hinduism sees man as a subject not an object, and that man's consciousness reflects the consciousness of the supreme spirit.[5] The point is made that these religions all have their individual perception of the human person.

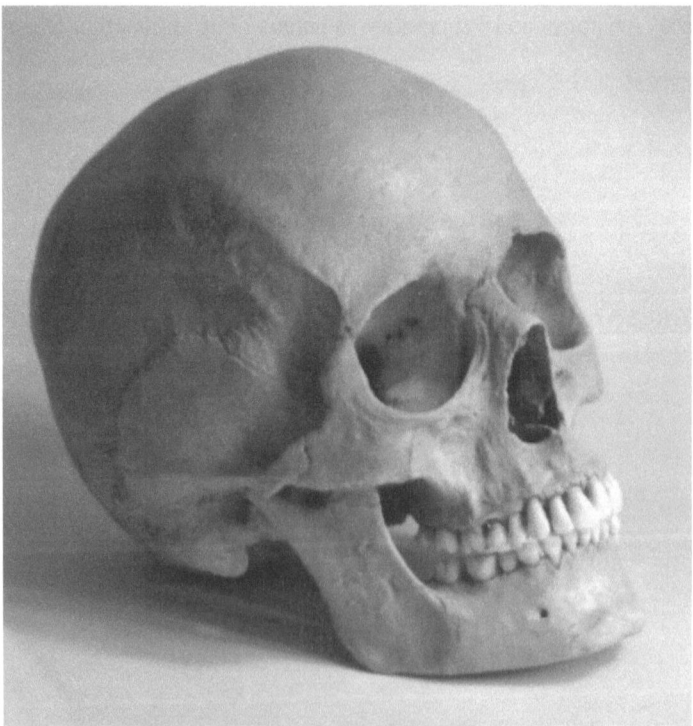

Figure 2.2. The Scientific View of Humans

There is no one scientific interpretation of the human person. Scientific interpretations of human beings are also not quite unified. There is a biological perspective, a physiological perspective, and an anthropological perspective. Science distinguishes between humans and other creatures based on our "advanced anatomical and physiological complexity" and "more elaborate behavioral patterns."[6] Liao (2013) states that even though the human body has been painstakingly and carefully studied and catalogued, it remains mysteriously unknown at many different levels.

Titus draws a conclusion on what it means to be human, however, which has great significance for us as we attempt to address human multiculturalism and its impact on the American educational system. He states that any purportedly comprehensive interpretation of man that neglects or ignores his ideas and ideals, or neglects his self-consciousness, "his power of abstract thought, his powers of ethical discrimination and aesthetic appreciation, and his need for worship and companionship is incomplete and inadequate."[7]

This view lends itself to a holistic view of the human person. These insights compel this work to go a step further to investigate the ethical, aesthetic, and religious dimension of the human person who is involved in the educational process.

Considering the insights from Titus, let's attempt a definition of the human person as "a biological being, who is inherently spiritual as well as culturally determined." To be human, therefore, would involve an attempt to fully articulate our biological, spiritual, and cultural attributes into one functional unit, called personality, which is able to be creative, reflective, and sociable.

A question that must be addressed in light of this definition of the human person, therefore, is "What does it mean to be a human being within the educational process, either as a learner or as a teacher?"

The Learner as a Social Being

Every child in the classroom comes from a social setting called *family*.[8] In the twenty-first-century America, the definition of family has changed drastically. The nineteenth and early twentieth centuries' definition of family was father, mother, and children. In the latter half of the twentieth century, the family was beginning to be gradually redefined, as divorce became a normal part of life in society.

Many children in the classroom began to come from homes made up of a mother, a stepfather, with both biological and step-siblings. Some have come from homes with father, stepmother, and step-siblings. Yet others were being raised by a single mother or single father. Some children were raised by grandparents, either because biological parents were incarcerated or deemed incompetent to raise them due to one social problem or another.

Toward the turn of the twenty-first century, we began to grapple with the question of gay and lesbian parenting. Today it is no longer an issue, as gays and lesbians are both adopting and raising children. The definition of family as we knew it has changed forever. This shift in social patterns has generated lots of arguments from both the conservative and liberal fronts. The former calls for a return to the original definition of family, while the later calls for a complete overhaul of social norms and expectations, to widen them to be more inclusive of these new forms and expressions of family. The liberal approach has called for a restructuring of educational curriculum to ensure a fair representation of the diversity that defines our twenty-first-century society.

Whereas the religious conservative view has lots of historic validity to it, as some of the factors that have led to the new forms of family reflect a departure from the religious and moral norms that formed the foundation of this society, a learner-centered pedagogy calls for a critical look at the implications of these shifts for the school child.

Does a child being raised in a gay or lesbian family see any oddity in the structure of his or her family? The argument may be stretched one way or the other. Should the classroom be the context for approving or disapproving one family structure over another? Again, the argument may be stretched even further. A more important question would be whether every child, irrespective of his or her family structure, has a right to be in the classroom and to be taught well. To this question, it would be odd to hear a negative response.

The question should therefore be how does the learner-centered classroom provide every child a safe and healthy learning environment, void of the intrusions of the divergent social views that influence the widening structure of the family? This is the task that today's educators must confront. Learning takes place in a social context, and fortunately or unfortunately, the American society happens to be the most divergent social arrangement of our time. Is it possible then to work toward synergy amid our diversity?

The questions raised in this chapter may never find one answer that fits all situations. These may be questions that would have to be answered within the collective arrangement of the school communities and their value systems. This may be one area in which the original community-oriented school governance that formed the educational structures of America becomes our best court of appeal.

Communities must be empowered to explore what constitutes the best interest of their constituents, without violating the rights of the minorities. Is there a way the interest of both the majority and the minority can be protected? These are questions that must be continuously asked as every stakeholder in a school site collaborates to find lasting solutions to these social problems. The idea of the learner as a social being will come up again for discussion.

The Learner as a Cultural Being

A few years ago, the topic of Ebonics as an alternative language for African-American students took the forefront in newspapers and radio/television broadcasts as people sought to find its place in the U.S. educational contexts. The significance of this debate does not rest exclusively on the problems posed by the uniqueness of the African-American version of the English language but reflects an acknowledgment that the African-American culture is distinct and different from the mainstream Anglo-Saxon Protestant culture.

The irony of that conversation was that the African-American population was split along lines of those who were for and those who were against the movement toward recognizing Ebonics as a language. That split anchored on the issue of cultural identity and how people wanted to be known and identified. Cultural identity theory therefore goes beyond issues around an individual's identity and socialization process to engage issues of cultural capital that one needs for survival and advancement in a given society.[9]

The American society is a mosaic of cultures. Right from the birth of this nation, diversity was its very essence. The Native Americans who had roamed the land centuries before the Europeans arrived were themselves a diverse group of people. They were made up of many different ethnicities with different languages, cultures, and social arrangements. The Europeans who came to the New World were homogeneous only for a short while. No sooner had they settled down than another flock of Europeans from the West joined the Anglo-Saxon flock that made up the earliest immigrants.

Over the years, events in Eastern Europe brought in Eastern Europeans as well. With the slave trade, the Africans were brought in to become part of the manpower that gave this nation its social arrangement, government, and economic structure. With the discovery of gold, different peoples from all over the world, some from as far away as China, made their way to the United States. With the construction of the transcontinental railroad, the Chinese came in even larger numbers.

As for the Spanish-speaking Americans, considering the fact that California and Texas were part of Mexico, it is difficult to regard them as immigrant groups. This confronts us with one certain reality, namely, that the

United States of America is and has always been the land of a divergent group of peoples.

One of the most disconcerting elements of contemporary educational structures remains the inability of some educators to come to terms with the diversity of our land and its educational environment. A learner-centered pedagogy does not call for mere tolerance because the language of tolerance is insulting and disrespectful of the many Americans of different ethnicities whose ancestors have paid high prices in war, servitude, death, and extreme hardships to make this country what it is today.

All Americans have a right to be seen as Americans and respected for theirs and the contributions of their ancestors to this great nation. The right language, therefore, is that of inclusion and equal opportunity. A learner-centered pedagogy must come to terms with the right of every child in the American classroom to be there and to be taught well to maximize his or her full potential. Instruction must be provided in the language and format that is most comprehensible to the child, enabling that child to achieve the desired academic goal.

The United States' history is filled with struggles and conflicts between different ethnicities since the founding of this nation: whites versus Indians; Western versus Eastern, Central, and Southern Europeans; whites versus Hispanics; and Hispanics versus African Americans. These are struggles and conflicts that must come to an end in the twenty-first century for us to build a unified nation. These are struggles and conflicts that must be conspicuously absent in the American classrooms of the twenty-first century.

In U.S. society, teachers are the frontline workers in the program of acculturating newcomers to American society. Outside of their immediate homes, for some students, the teacher is the first and only adult that has any role in influencing their adaptation to their new community, the United States. Given the fact that teachers know, to some extent, that this is their responsibility, they tend to adopt one of two approaches to doing the job.

Teachers as Assimilators

Some teachers see themselves as agents of assimilation. They uphold the melting pot ideology, in which the student is expected to get rid of everything ethnic and become "American" as the claim goes. Students whose beliefs and behaviors do not match those of successful mainstream students are seen as lacking in "ability, prior knowledge, motivation, or communication skills."[10] This mind-set often leads to disrespect and low academic expectations for these students, which consequently leads these students to develop feelings of rejection, low self-esteem, and consequently poor academic achievements.

Teachers as Accommodators

When teachers see themselves as accommodators, they tend to make accommodations in their teaching to facilitate learning for the non-mainstream students. They tend to exhibit respect toward these students and this translates to the students seeing themselves as capable, lacking nothing other than to catch up with the way things are said and done in this new culture. This is a classroom that has the interest and development of the child as its primary commitment, not the perpetuation of a dominant culture, which is seen as being in competition with other microcultures. The teacher's role is not that of cultural police but that of an educator, a friend, and an ally to the learner who is on a journey toward self-development and self-actualization.

For a teacher to effectively educate students from diverse backgrounds, the teacher must first come to terms with his or her humanity, his or her cultural identity, and then go the next step of affirming the humanity of the students in his or her classroom as well as affirming their individual cultural identities.

In order to attain this goal, one of the exercises I take my teacher candidates through is a cultural autobiography project titled "Who Am I in My Culture?" In this project students take time to research their cultural heritage as well as the other cultural influences that have made them who they are. They write their autobiography and come to class with it, along with important artifacts that represent their cultures. These are shared with the whole class, and this ends up being one of the most intriguing parts of our diversity class. In the section below, I share a few samples of what these teacher candidates have written, and we will also discuss them.

WHO AM I IN MY CULTURE?

All of the candidates responding to this question are student teachers who are engaging the question of their cultural identity within the first two weeks of their first diversity class in a teacher education program. As you will come to discover through the write-ups, some candidates already have a very broad understanding of culture and are very much in tune with their cultural identity.

The most revealing aspect of these narratives is the fact that somehow within those first two weeks of class, these individuals come to terms with the fact that they possess unique cultural identities that make them who they are within the larger U.S. society. With the permission of these students, these narratives are presented here to illustrate the strength of individual cultural experiences and how much they help in defining who we are.

Narrative Number One: Meet Marcos Garcia

Hello, I am the product of parents who met in the vineyards of Ukiah, California. I am a brown boy in a White world, ashamed of my skin and of my Spanish-speaking father.

I am the one who answered a Spanish question in English. I am the one who wished I could be anyone but me. I am the one who, in high school, was Mexican to the White kids and American to the brown kids. To which side do I lay claim? I am the one whose parents said, "Follow your dreams, you don't want to work like we do." I am the one who worked construction with my father and found college to be a better place. His hard work withered the feelings of embarrassment.

I am the one who took a Mexican/American literature course and found out that Mexican people actually wrote books and that I was not alone with my feelings. I am the one who minored in Chicano Studies, read book after book, and finally found something to shatter the pretenses. I am the one who is proud of being Chicano and refuses to use the term *hisPANIC*.

I am the one who does not need to eat with a fork, tortillas will do, gracias. I am the one everyone looks at when they need a Spanish translator. Yes, I do speak Spanish by the way. I am the one who went to film school to make films that showcased the realities of my culture. I am the one who, at the time, was the only Chicano directing rap music videos.

I am the one who continues to write in an effort to get our stories up on the silver screen. I am the one who got into teaching to show students that they can be what they want to be, that they are not limited to the stereotypes and menial jobs the media portrays. I am the one who needs to lead by example and instill in my students the power of having dreams and the satisfaction of realizing them.

I am a son, a brother, an uncle, a nino, a chicano, a writer, a teacher. I am Marcos Angelberto Garcia. Pleased to meet you.

Man is never closer to himself than when he is close to his community. This is the best way to illustrate how I began to transition from a shameful sense of history to a proud past. A variety of people and experiences have helped shape my thoughts and feelings over the years. However, the browning of my skin begins with my parents.

I remember the instance that laid the first coat. I was sixteen; riding in the bed of a trusty red Toyota pick-up truck with a plastic shell nestled over my head. My family and I were returning from a Sunday afternoon at the Redondo Beach Pier. My brother and sister rode alongside me, exhausted. Suddenly, I heard my father beat the horn and pound the brakes. An Anglo man nearly sideswiped our truck. My father yelled for him to watch where he was going in his Spanish accent. The man retaliated with, "You fucking wetback!" WETBACK! Wetback! All other sounds faded to a whisper. Wetback?

It sounded so heavy, so unbearable; it forced me to breathe a rapid breath, like I was suffocating. I remember wondering, *who are we*? I knew then I did not belong to an American community.

Other incidents also occurred to family and neighbors that caused me to question who I was. But my parents were always there to instill in me with confidence, "If they want to call us wetbacks, so what? We know who we are!" They made sure to let me know people will call us names but never be sorry for who I am. This is the price they paid to live a better life, one out of the fields and integrated into an American society. I was beginning to listen with the darkening of my skin.

I then entered my senior year in high school. I had to take English 1B with Frank Zepeda. He was different from any other teacher on campus. He was Mexican. He spoke to us in Spanglish, called us "chuntaros" and we liked it. It was strange to see someone who looked like a relative teaching a class, especially mine. He helped us believe in ourselves as young Chicanos. He spoke about things that happened in our homes. He was one of us. He once wrote on one of my essays, "I like your writing style."

The simplest of comments can last a lifetime. He made me realize that anyone in our community could succeed if they had the desire. I went on to enroll at Mt. San Antonio College a few years later. At the urging of a friend, I registered for Mexican/American Literature. It was literally shocking to find out how many books were written by Latinos. I felt betrayed by the American public school system for not allowing me the opportunity to be aware these books ever existed. Professor Julian Medina challenged us to debate issues and topics facing the Chicano community. We read books, poems, watched films, and discussed the feelings of the authors. Some shared my sentiments. I was relieved to know I was not alone. I was not the only one without knowledge of my past. I began to look at the people in my community with a new familiarity. There was hope for me yet to still grow a shade darker.

I later transferred to California State University, Long Beach, to major in film production. After the eye-opening experience in the literature class, I also majored in Chicano studies. I needed to learn about the people who opened the doors for me to succeed, about where my mother and father came from and why they hold their beliefs. I began to learn the other side of history and what was done to the people of Mexico.

I learned about injustice and racism and why people think my father is a wetback and why he will never be one. Again, I felt betrayed by the school system. Why do we not know at least a portion of our history? Why do we not know about the origins of our community? The more I read, the closer I grew to my community; the closer I grew to knowing who I am, being browned by the rays of experience.

I do not feel this transition could have happened any other way. It could not have happened sooner; it could not have happened at the urging of others. It had to take place within the realm of my own destiny. I now know the history of the faces in my community. I know the struggles, the pride, and the will to survive. I know because I am one of them.

This piece is one of the most revealing pieces written by these student teachers. I chose to preserve the original names because I believe that this is a story worth telling in its truest form. Marcos did not only write about his cultural identity, he went further to elaborate on his journey toward that cultural identity. The realism that this piece presents to us is the struggle of cultural identity that children born into immigrant homes go through as they grow up in U.S. society.

Such struggles are rarely considered a major issue by the schools and educators, yet this case demonstrates the extent to which they shape the individuals' lives and perspectives. The crises of cultural self-awareness are major issues that must begin to be addressed if multicultural education is to take a deep root in our educational settings.

Cultural awareness and self-identity is not a struggle for immigrant American children only, it is a major issue that other groups of American children deal with. A white teacher candidate wrote concerning her own cultural identity. Some of these names have been altered to protect the characters, so let's call her Sherri.

Narrative Number Two: Meet Sherri

My grandparents were immigrants from both Poland and Italy.
They came to Ellis Island at the turn of the twentieth century.
Matthew and Sophia Mocniak settled in a Pennsylvania coal-mining town.
Pneumonia claimed Matthew soon after, from his labors underground.
Pascal and Nelie Pacino stayed in New York to raise a family.
They built a thriving business in Bronx's "Little Italy."

My parents met each other in their melting-pot neighborhood.
Mike and Josephina both excelled by working as hard as they could.
Their honeymoon was a stay out West, where my father built his career.
He became a most sought after, brilliant aerospace engineer.
Orange, California, was the suburb chosen to make their home.

My two brothers and I had plenty of freedom, and lots of space to roam.
As I reflect back on the experiences that are ingrained in me,
I see a comfortable childhood, full of opportunities.
I was born in 1960, and given a soap-opera star's name.
Angela Diane Mocniak via Diane Cannon's fame.

> Religious faith, love, and togetherness created family unity.
> Caring for and working within, strengthened our community.
>
> Taught to respect our elders, and those of every color, shape, and size.
> We were exposed to the downtrodden, their plight to recognize.
> I married John at nineteen, too young many did say.
> I knew he was the "one for me," and we are together to this day.
>
> My husband is a mixture of ethnicities gently stirred.
> As for our two daughters, the lines have all been blurred.
> We too moved to the country, to raise our family, with hopes
> that we could capture some of the ways it used to be.

Here we see a classic case of a descendant of a set of European immigrants, who captured the American dream by all its definition, and whose descendants have also done very well. This woman would be the typical American girl; yet, she confronts one glaring truth about her culture and heritage, "the lines have all been blurred." The fact of cultural identity within the American white population is more challenging today than among many other groups.

In a typical class of fifteen to twenty students, more than 60 percent will be white. When we undertake this exercise of cultural self-discovery, more than 70 percent of these white students will confess to the lines being blurred as much as racial and cultural identity is concerned.

For most of these students, cultural identity is no longer anchored on a European descent since the European blood has mixed with African, Native American, Jewish, and sometimes Asian blood; instead they have carved out for themselves a new cultural identity, which is uniquely theirs and uniquely American. While some readers may be tempted to see this as a negative development, it may be necessary to consider that maybe herein lies the strength of being truly American. The melting pot ideology, which has been espoused in the history of this country, may be somewhat of a reality, and may have given America her unique cultural identity.

Americans of all ethnicities may attempt to trace their cultural heritage to somewhere outside the American shores, but there has been such a mingling within America that our identities can no longer be exclusively defined in terms of our non-American ancestry.

The next case is from an African-American woman. She has come to terms with the reality of her cultural identity in a very unique way.

Narrative Number Three: Meet Reygyndta

When you examine your place in your culture, a good first place to begin is your name. While your name can reveal your ethnicity or culture, how you choose to pronounce it reveals even more about how you *feel* about your cultural background. And then there are those names that just leave you guessing. That's my name. My birth name is Reygyndta Vian Mari Warna Wertlow. My name is a significant part of my culture because African Americans value creativity. Being different is praiseworthy in dress style, music trends, and even name choice. It would be unheard of in African-American culture to look to a name book, except to see what had already been taken.

Like many African-American women, my mother just made up my name. There is no other name like it, though the sounds are not in themselves unique. Unfortunately, the creativity of African-American culture that has been displayed through creative names is experiencing a backlash. Some of the creative names have been seen as absurd and have been ridiculed in the public.

Whereas having a unique name was at one time a symbol of pride, it has, in mainstream American culture, become more of a burden and a stigma. These creative names are now considered "ghetto," evoking images of welfare mothers and illiterate children. Anyone with hopes of professional success has to now seriously consider how their names affect people's perceptions of their abilities and intellect. Names like Shavonia and Tyloquiesha are not only unique, but they also carry a stigma.

For the most part, I have been able to evade such considerations. For almost all of my life, I have gone by "Rey" because people have a hard time saying *Reygyndta*.

The second thing that my name tells about my culture is the significance of the matriarchs. I am named after two of my grandmothers, Warna and Mari, giving honor and homage to the generations that came before my mother.

In African-American culture, the matriarchs are very important. The strength that African-American women have had to possess in order to survive and protect their families in a White male–dominated society has become a fable. "Being strong" is a noble characteristic and a compliment that every African-American woman would want to have (true for all groups, I'm sure, but especially true in African-American culture).

It is this name that I believe truly sums up who I am in my culture. My husband's last name, Sirakavit, is Thai, though he is not (another interesting, but unrelated story). And, the middle name that we both chose to take is Badilika, which is Swahili for "to be changed." My name is multicultural—it reflects my personal and familial heritage, and my distant ancestors, but also an acceptance of other groups.

Living in Southern California, I have been blessed with the opportunity to be immersed in many different cultures: from East LA (mostly Latino) to Claremont (mostly White) to Baldwin Village (mostly African American). Each of these groups has shaped my cultural identity. So, I like to think that my new name reflects, to a greater extent, the multicultural nature of my life and experiences. While I am African American culturally, my culture is more than just African American.

In this short write-up, Reygyndta gives us a classic case of one who has come to a full grasp of the dynamics of her cultural identity. Here is an African-American woman who goes beyond the conventional racial identity to seek a definition of her cultural identity deep within the experiential, historical, as well as environmental factors that have shaped her life and that of her cultural group. This is a dimension that most Americans are reluctant to explore. Those who venture into this sphere, however, are mostly those who have suffered one kind of social deprivation or the other, which was based on their ethnic or cultural identity, especially, those who are unable to "pass for white."[11]

The question that arises, therefore, is whether we must wait for crises and oppressions to arouse the desire to establish our cultural identity. The beauty of the American cultural landscape is that it is a mosaic. We have those forces and principles that hold us together as one nation under God, and we also have those unique characteristics, as well as heritage, that provide for the variety that makes America so beautiful.

Cultural diversity is indeed beautiful. The beauty of Old Town Pasadena, in the San Gabriel Valley of California, can be found in the variety of restaurants that attract thousands of people from across the southland on a daily basis: Thai restaurants, Indian restaurants, Chinese, Cantonese, Italian, Mexican, French, Armenian—just name it. Each one thrives, patronized by Americans of a variety of ethnicities and races, suggesting that there is more to being American than the skin color and ethnic heritage to which we cling. The next candidate, a student teacher of Asian descent, seems to be arriving at a state of equilibrium in terms of her cultural identity.

Narrative Number Four: Meet Kim

Chopsticks, respecting of elders, piano, In-N-Out hamburgers, shopping malls, independence—such is the mixture of words that describe my eclectic background. When I think about my culture, I think Korean, American, Korean-American. These two heritages have somehow fused together to make up who I am, to become my own unique heritage and form a generation of people almost like me. When I was younger, my schoolmates would ask me, "Where are you from?" To which I could not give an answer. If I said I was "American," they would further prod, "But then how come your eyes are so different?" Those students who were not as nice to pose questions merely jeered, "Go back to the country you came from!" I did not know how to respond back to them that I was from the country of America. I had been born and raised in Los Angeles. I was at a loss to explain myself to my ignorant peers. Attending an all-White, middle-class private school did not help much. During my elementary and junior high years, I only remember about six other Asian students, all of whom were Korean like me.

My brother left after sixth grade to attend the public middle school; I always thought part of his reason for leaving was because of the racism he faced. The other Asian students also phased out eventually. I, however, felt comfortable at my school. But it was not until high school, when I attended a public high school, that I started acknowledging and interacting with other minority students in a school setting. The high school I attended had an ethnically diverse population of students.

Going on to college, I took courses in Asian-American and ethnic studies, and finally started appreciating my background and culture for its full worth and value. I had found my identity. I have visited Korea a couple of times recently. I always feel like a foreigner there. Even though my facial features and hair color make me fit into the homogenous mixture, and though I can speak the language quite fluently, I have never felt at home. On the other hand, in America, I am one of many minorities. Yet, for the most part, I feel like this country is my home, the place where I belong. I feel accepted and valued, and when I face ignorance, I like to teach rather than react negatively.

Asian Americans are victims of the "model-minority" myth. And even though I do play piano, and though I study diligently and sometimes drive recklessly, I am not particularly adept at math and science, nor do I know martial arts or consider myself exotic looking. If you were to ask me who I was within my culture, I would say I am "myself."

I have been influenced by American cultural traditions and ideals, such as American food and independence, but I have also been influenced by my Asian cultural values, such as respecting my elders, having a hard work ethic, and the importance of family. These two cultures have fluidly joined together to form my own culture, an Asian-American (or Korean-American) culture, and it is within this culture that I find who I am.

In the United States, we have come into an age where our ethnicities and races must fuse with the other cultural factors that are uniquely American to define our individual cultural identities. That process may be easier for some, because they have a lighter skin tone; all of us must, nevertheless, be prepared to confront this process of engaging our evolving new cultural identities as we all thrive to build "one indivisible nation under God." The activities below will help you to interact personally with the issues raised in this chapter.

QUESTIONS AND APPLICATION

Activity: Who Am I in My Culture?

Based on the insights gained from chapter 1, articulate a personal statement of your cultural identity. Describe your cultural identity beginning with your heritage and the cultural and worldview influences that have shaped you into becoming who you are today. Describe how your cultural identity will impact the way you function as a K–12 teacher.

Review Questions

a. Compare the different cultural experiences presented in this chapter. What similarities and differences do you observe across the responses?
b. What are the distinguishing elements that make each of these individuals Americans? How do their ethnic roots enhance or detract from their American identity?
c. What other ways can K–12 teachers aid their students in their struggle for cultural self-awareness? Develop an action plan you can use in helping your students as they navigate through their personal struggles for cultural identity.

Strategies for Application

The following activities can be used in applying the principles and lessons of this chapter to a K–12 classroom situation.

1. *Grades K–6 Classroom Setting*: Students can work with their parents to write their family history, identifying history of immigration to the United States, cultural mixes and intermarriages that may have taken place along their ancestral lines. These papers can be presented in class with parents (for grades K–3 students) or alone by students (for grades 4–6 students). This will allow for sharing of cultural heritage and family history with the whole class, creating a positive attitude toward cultural differences.

2. *Grades 7–12 Classroom Setting*: Students can research their cultural and family history, write research papers, and do murals, or other kinds of special projects to showcase their history and cultural heritage. This could be a way to excite students or their families to begin a family tree project. Family history/cultural event day could be organized with multicultural food and exhibition of their projects.

Chapter Three

Engaging the American Cultural Mosaic

Chapter Objectives:

This chapter presents critical analysis of the American culture. At the end of the chapter, readers will be able to do the following:

1. Conceptualize the American culture as a mosaic
2. Describe the historical factors that have shaped the American culture
3. Explain the interactive nature of cultural structures and their effects on the dynamic shifts that take place within cultures and worldviews

WHAT IS CULTURE?

To properly understand the concept of culture, we must begin by articulating a clear definition of the word. Culture is a concept that has been defined in different ways by many different interests and disciplines. Whereas a variety of definitions abound for culture from different fields and disciplines, the desire here is not to compare definitions but to isolate those that make the concept of culture very clear and appropriate for our context.

One of the definitions of culture that stands out within the field of multicultural education is by Sonia Nieto (2004), who defined it as the values, traditions, social relationships, and worldviews created, shared, and transformed by a group of people. This definition captured many of the varied elements that make up culture. Generally speaking, however, the field of cultural anthropology tends to provide a better and more precise definition of culture.

Two anthropologists, Kroeber and Kluckhohn (1952), presented a definition that provides a very clear insight into this concept of culture,

> Culture consists of patterns, explicit and implicit, of and for behavior acquired and transmitted by symbols, constituting the distinctive achievement of human groups, including their embodiments in artifacts; the essential core of culture consists of traditional (i.e., historically derived and selected) ideas and especially their attached values; culture systems may, on the one hand, be considered as products of action, on the other hand as conditioning elements of further action.[1]

It is important to note a concept of culture here as implicit and explicit patterns of and for behavior, distinctive achievements, artifacts, ideas, and their attached values. These concepts of culture may not lend themselves readily to a regular and more contemporary definition of culture, but they present profound insights into what culture really means. It will be very appropriate to analyze this definition in order to appreciate its practicality and utility.

THE AMERICAN CULTURE AS A MOSAIC

American culture, as used in this section, should be seen as representing the United States, the continental America. Given the plurality of the American ethnic makeup, one would rightly question the validity of a reference to "American culture." The whole concept of American culture must be seen as pluralistic in its essence. American culture is more of a mosaic.

Within a larger umbrella of American cultural mosaic, there is a macroculture, which serves as the glue or the frame that holds the rest of the microcultures in place. This macroculture is essentially the American flavor of the Anglo-Saxon Protestant culture, which was the dominant culture of colonial America and has continued to be the dominant culture of the modern-day United States. Its dominance should not suggest the exclusion or marginalization of the rest of the microcultures, which in earlier days were Irish, German, Scottish, Polish, Italian, African, Chinese, Japanese, and Native American (not an exhaustive list).

The contemporary face of American microcultures reveals a numerous array of cultures representing peoples from all countries on earth. The idea of American culture as a mosaic is portrayed in the fact that English remains the dominant language of commerce and trade as well as government, while the validity of other languages as credible and valuable for commerce and diplomatic relations is affirmed.

The American ideas and ideals that govern the way things are done here, such as freedom, equality, equal access to opportunities, capitalism, free enterprise, and what have you, remain the same over the more than two hundred years that this nation has been in existence. When second-generation immigrants change their languages and lifestyles, they mostly adopt this mainstream Anglo-Saxon Protestant culture rather than another microculture like Italian, or Irish, or Taiwanese.

As immigrants and their children acculturate, they tend to keep their ancestral cultures while adopting the mainstream culture. This tendency toward biculturalism is very much a dynamic of the American immigrant population and not a rejection of the mainstream culture. A cross-section of the American cultural matrix may, therefore, reveal a plurality of cultures, yet each microculture is only one small face within a larger mosaic glued together by principles and practices that were established under a predominantly Anglo-Saxon Protestant culture. In that respect we can confidently speak about American culture without necessarily contradicting ourselves.

To fully understand this macroculture that serves as the frame on which the rest of the American systems as well as microcultures hang, we need to look at American culture in light of the definition given by Kroeber and Kluckhohn (1952), as patterns of behavior, symbols, and the distinctive achievements of human groups, ideas, actions, and the products of action.[2]

The American Culture as Patterns of Behaviors/Practices

First, let's look at culture as consisting of patterns "of behavior, as well as providing patterns for behavior." Within every cultural group there are certain patterns of behavior that are unique to them. For many generations, when an American is walking down a street of Paris or Frankfurt, for example, an average European has a way of knowing that the individual is an American even before the American individual opens his or her mouth. This may no longer be as prominent today as it used to be due to a growing global trend of Americanization.

More often than not, Americans carry themselves in a way that distinguishes them. They are often assertive and walk with broad shoulders. Americans know and demand their rights, which may seem too assertive and offensive to some non-Americans.[3] Some other cultures would be more yielding even when their rights are being infringed upon, but an average American would not tolerate any appearance of humiliation or an infringement of his or her rights. This is a pattern of behavior that distinguishes them from others. Often they do this to a fault.

During a tour of Victoria Falls in the year 2000, a Zimbabwean tourist guide talked about how someone often falls to his or her death into the gorge in the waterfalls each year. According to him, 99 percent of those who fall are usually Americans. The reason being that they are usually more daring, often going far beyond the boundaries clearly marked out for tourists. This could be a result of curiosity and a daredevil attitude that characterizes most Americans—another pattern of behavior. Guggenheim (2010), in the film *Waiting for Superman*, put it more positively when he said that American students are outperformed in all areas by students in comparable nations—except in self-confidence.

Indeed every cultural group has behavior patterns that distinguish them from the others. A Nigerian friend told this story about walking into a Lebanese shop in Mali West Africa and the shopkeeper sat leisurely in his seat, not bothering that he had a customer.

After walking around for a few minutes and noticing that the storekeeper was not going to come and assist him, my friend walked up to him and asked, "Mr. Man, are you selling these items or are they just for display. Haven't you noticed you have a customer?" The shopkeeper got up from his seat and said, "You must be a Nigerian. Nobody from around here will speak to me like that." He was right because patterns of behavior in Nigeria can be significantly different from other parts of Africa.

Glenn et al. (2016) make the point that most human behaviors are acquired as a result of learning from other humans through observation and explicit instruction. So it must be noted that enduring cultural behaviors reflect purposeful handing over of certain ideas, behaviors, and practices from one generation to the next.

The American Culture as Symbols

A second focus within this definition is the idea of culture as transmitted through symbols and constituting the significant distinctiveness of human groups. Every cultural group has its own symbols that distinguish it from the rest of the world. Each country has its own flag, which is the most commonly shared symbol across the world. Other symbols, however, distinguish some cultures in a unique way. The Statue of Liberty has become a symbol of American freedom. Anywhere the image of that statue is seen across the world, it clearly identifies America, and no other nation. On a lighter mood, the hamburger has also become a cultural symbol that signifies the American fast-paced life.

America is one of the few countries of the world where it is acceptable for people to be walking along the street with a cup of Starbucks coffee or a soda can and possibly a hamburger to go with it, or driving with one hand and eating with the other. Some other cultures have etiquettes that despise such behaviors. On the flip side, many French people and former French colonies still observe a two-hour afternoon lunch, which goes with a siesta. An average American would look at that as a reckless waste of productivity and manpower. Life seems slower paced in many European cities (such as Zurich, Paris, Amsterdam, even London) compared to America and its fast-paced life.

The American Culture as Human Achievements

Every country of the world has museums that are filled with statues, monuments, images, publications, and write-ups about national heroes and cultural icons. What makes individual heroes and icons can vary from society to society, yet each society is unique. Whereas certain accomplishments carry lots of recognition among some peoples, it may not attract any serious attention from others.

For many countries in Africa, Central America, and South America, soccer players have the highest honor a sports person could possibly get. People in the United States, however, honor football, baseball, and basketball players, games that are hardly noticed in most of the countries that value soccer. Within different cultural contexts, human achievements tell us about the people's cultures and ways of life.

The history and culture of the United States have been heavily influenced and shaped by the American Revolutionary War. Monuments have been erected for George Washington, the Revolutionary War leader and first U.S. president. The significance of the achievements of Washington and his comrades can be seen in the American spirit of fearlessness, tenacity, and courage.

America does not seem to shy away from wars because there is a legacy of victory as well as the need for self-preservation. In fact, it is said that the earliest American flag had the symbol of a rattlesnake on it, sending a message that says, "Don't step on me or you will be bitten." That message shaped America's response to Pearl Harbor and the most recent event of September 11, 2001.[4]

A monument was also erected to honor Abraham Lincoln, America's leader in one of the most difficult times in history. Lincoln's bravery, ingenuity, and leadership skills were the primary factors that led to the North's victory during the Civil War, as well as the fact that America was able to forge ahead as one nation despite that war.

More recently a monument was commissioned to honor Martin Luther King Jr. At the commissioning ceremony, U.S. president George W. Bush, in his speech, stated that it was not coincidental that Martin Luther King Jr.'s memorial was being erected in the same area where both Washington's and Lincoln's memorials stand. He stated that whereas Washington fought for the promise of America's freedom and Lincoln extended that freedom to all Americans, Martin Luther King Jr. made that promise a reality. In effect, therefore, each one of those monuments must be seen as a celebration of human achievements within the larger U.S. history.

Apart from these monuments, we have all kinds of halls of fame—Pro Football Hall of Fame, NBA Broadcasting Hall of fame, and the Musicians Hall of Fame, just to name a few. We have the Hollywood Walk of Fame, which celebrates the achievement of many individuals who have made significant contributions to the entertainment industry. It is part of the American culture to celebrate human achievements.

The American Culture as Sets of Ideas and Belief Systems

Some of the most significant ideas that have shaped the American cultural landscape include the ideas of freedom, equality, and happiness.[5] The earliest Europeans who came to America came in search of freedom, and that idea of freedom was behind the resistance to the English throne, which led to the American Revolution.

The American concept of freedom reflects in the way an average American lives his or her life. One of the cultural shocks that immigrants from Asia, Africa, and South America face on coming to America is the extent of freedom that America's children enjoy. The sway of authority with which parents from developing countries rule their families is drastically reduced once they step onto American soil. Individual freedom is a highly priced asset, and American culture respects it more than anything else.

On the matter of equality, whereas Americans can be rightfully accused of scoring very poorly in the historical past in terms of human rights and social equality, it has emerged in the last few decades at the forefront of the global battle for equity and fair play. This progress is possible because the U.S. Bill of Rights espouses the idea of equality.

The American way of life assumes that "[a]ll men are created equal, and endowed with such inalienable rights as life, liberty, and the pursuit of happiness" (First Amendment to U.S. Constitution). This idea of equality has been the bedrock on which the structures of equality and the battles for human rights that have become part of everyday life in America have been built. It is an ideology that has indeed shaped the America of the twenty-first century, and continues to do so.

Lastly, most writers rarely pay close attention to the idea of happiness. This ideology, however, is fundamental to the American way of life. Is it not significant that this country may be the only country on earth that included the idea of happiness in its Bill of Rights? Americans have grown to love a life of pursuance of happiness. We love big cars, big homes, and big television screens—anything that can make us happy.

The sad part of the cultural influence of this idea of happiness is the effect it has had on the family structure in recent years. Men and women are no longer willing to work on difficult relationships. People quickly exit a marriage relationship once they sense that their happiness is threatened (sometimes before their lives are).

Kroeber and Kluckhohn's definition of culture, therefore, presents us with a very exhaustive look at culture, which takes it beyond the conventional concepts of traditions, beliefs, and practices. Based on their definition, we can conclude that a more precise way to look at culture would be to conceptualize it as *a given set of ideas, belief systems, worldviews, practices, and artifacts that define a group of people as well as distinguishing them from others*.

A CROSS-SECTION OF THE AMERICAN CULTURAL ARRANGEMENT

Within any society, culture must be conceptualized as an arrangement, a structure, and an organized system. The characteristics of culture include the facts that it is learned, shared, adaptable, and dynamic.[6] Culture is made up of internal and superficial elements, concrete and symbolic elements. The superficial and symbolic aspects of the culture often deceive visitors to new cultural arrangements and they fail to probe its internal and concrete aspects. Strict discipline and engagement is required for newcomers to a cultural arrangement for them to fully understand the intricacies of that setting.

In this work, however, we prefer to look at the elements or contents of culture as arranged in an intricate web of relationships. To fully understand culture, we need to look at it as one unit of an intricate set of arrangements, and then we will dissect it and look at each component based on its significance and merit, after which we will look at each one in relationship to the others.

Charles Kraft (1979) discussed cultural patterning and the centralization of worldview in this kind of arrangement. He identified four significant components of culture as religious structures, social structure, technological structure, and linguistic structure, with worldview as the core, which he labels the organizer of conceptualization (figure 3.1).

Whereas sociologists categorize religious and economic structures as well as political and family structures as parts of social institutions and structures, Kraft separated these structures and made social structure a category among others (religious, linguistic, and technological). It makes sense to speak of culture as a more embracing concept with social structure as the aspect that deals with family structures, regulation of human behaviors, values and norms, social relationships, associations, and other similar arrangements.

In this work, therefore, we have chosen to build on Kraft's work and attempt to conceptualize culture as a sphere with a core and six different components. The core is worldview, Kraft's organizer of conceptualizations.[7]

The components of culture are expanded to six in order to separate the political and economic substructures from the social, since these are very complex structures in and of themselves. Sociologists identify specific areas within which basic human needs are met in society; these include the family sector, the educational institutions, and the economic, religious, and political sectors.[8] According to these authors, the American social structure would

Figure 3.1. Charles Kraft's Cultural Patterns

show the presence of monogamy, along with Judeo-Christian values and norms, and the institutionalization of economic competition and of democratic political organizations as norm.[9]

Let's, therefore, look at the following substructures—religious, political, economic, linguistic, technological, and social arrangements—as structures that can enable us to engage the American culture and worldview. The web of cultural patterning that represents this is illustrated in figure 3.2.

The Structure of American Macroculture

In this section we will focus on the structure of the mainstream United States cultures, to which all Americans, regardless of race and ethnicity, subscribe. The substructure we have presented below (figure 3.2) represents this macroculture. In order to appreciate the unique significance of each substructure within this macroculture, we will engage each one as an individual part of the whole unit.

A group of sociologists wrote the following words just a few years ago: "[A] description of American social structure would indicate the presence of monogamy along with Judeo-Christian values and norms and the institutionalization of economic competition and of democratic political organizations."[10]

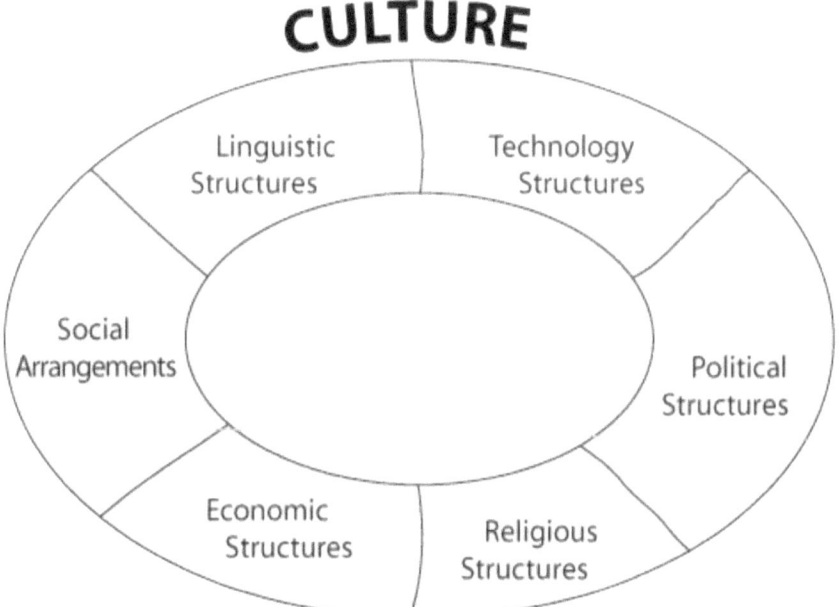

Figure 3.2. American Cultural Patterning

This statement is less than adequate in describing the American social structure, since along with the monogamous family structure, you have Mormon polygamist practices along with rampant divorces and remarriages, which can now be described as serial polygamy.

The Judeo-Christian values are presently challenged by a secular humanistic worldview that is pervading the American moral and spiritual landscape. These substructures—religious substructures, political substructures, economic substructures, linguistic substructures, technological substructures, and social arrangements—must then be examined in depth.

The U.S. Religious Substructure

Emile Durkheim (1915) presented a definition of religion that sees it as "a unified system of beliefs and practices relative to sacred things, that is so to say, things set apart and forbidden—beliefs and practices which unite into one single moral community called a Church, all those who adhere to them."[11] America of the twenty-first century is religiously pluralistic. The history of this nation points back to a beginning, which was steeped in Anglo-Saxon Protestant Christian heritage. This heritage, while still very strong and enduring, has gradually yielded to a more inclusive religious atmosphere in keeping with the espoused bill of rights, which entitles every American to a choice of religion without any governmental interference.

The Anglo-Saxon Protestant ethic, however, strongly influenced both the legal and political arrangements of America, and has remained a very strong influence. Along with it, today, are myriad eastern religions like Buddhism, Hinduism, Confucianism, Islam, and what have you. America of the twentieth century actually saw the birth of a new religious expression known as New Age movement, along with other ideologies that some have chosen to classify as religious despite strong objections from the adherents.

Such ideologies include the cults of American patriotism, atheism, secular humanism, and many other forms of philosophical ideologies that have become almost militant. America has, therefore, become a land where you have the right to worship anything you choose. America even floats an organized church of Satan.

Religious tolerance, therefore, should distinguish America from many other nations where citizens are restricted and compelled to adhere to specific religious traditions. Some fundamentalist Christians are always talking about a return to our Christian roots; such a return may be practically impossible given the unique cultural characteristics of the twenty-first-century America. America will continue to be a land of freedom of religious expression, and the dominance of one religion over the others may soon become impracticable.

Political Substructure

The American political system is a democratic setup that is rooted in representative government. Officeholders are empowered through an electoral process by the citizens (electorates) to serve, thus giving them legal mandate or rights to hold government offices and maintain public liberties.[12]

The idea of freedom has been established as the basic principle that led to the founding of this nation as well as a principle that led to the fighting and winning of the American Revolution. That principle set the stage for America's political arrangement. The U.S. Declaration of Independence stated, "We hold these truths to be self-evident, that all men are created equal, that they are endowed by their creator with certain unalienable Rights that among these are Life, Liberty and pursuit of Happiness."[13]

Americans pride themselves as being the architects of the modern democratic system of government. In the American Revolution they rejected the tyrannical sway of the British crown and set up their own government, raising an ordinary farmer and military general (George Washington) to a rank equal to that of kings, yet making sure he did not see himself as one.

The three arms of government (the executive, legislative, and judiciary) provide checks and balances, and ensure that the people continue to have a voice in the way their land is run. Abraham Lincoln later encapsulated the concept of democracy as the government of the people, by the people, and for the people.[14] This concept is very much American.

In the twenty-first century we have seen democracy at work in America as George W. Bush, in the wake of the terrorist activity of September 11, 2001, had to lobby the U.S. Congress to give him authorization before he could go to war against Iraq. Even though he was the chief executive, he needed to avoid a unilateral decision when it comes to putting America's young people in harm's way. The common citizens got involved in this decision process as many congressmen and congresswomen sent out questionnaires to their constituents to find out what they thought about going to war against Iraq before they could vote yes or no.

A few years ago, President Barack Obama backed away from attacking the Syrian army after Bashar al-Assad used chemical weapons, because the U.S. Congress would not give him an authorization to wage war against Syria. This is democracy at its best, and no country seems to exemplify these principles today the way America does.

The Economic Substructure

The concept of American freedom and independence is best embodied in the spirit of the Frontiers Movement: the fact that one individual would venture out with his family and set up a homestead in the middle of nowhere. The frontiersman could take this risk because he knew that when he tilled the land and planted his tobacco, corn, or cotton, he could harvest the farm proceed and keep the whole profit.

The American economic arrangement called capitalism is a liberating economic system. It is a major factor that has placed America at the forefront of international market economy. Some historians believe that all human actions, and consequently culture and social development, derive from a people's economic condition. This idea holds that "all social standing and political power is based on one's level of prosperity."[15] Individual ownership of property encourages adventure and economic initiatives.

The American marketplace is flooded with all levels of entrepreneurs. Through tax cuts and all kinds of incentives, the government continues to encourage the average American to enter the American marketplace as sellers, not just buyers. This is absent in many other countries where the line between the "haves" and "have-nots" has been drawn. Stories of rags-to-riches characterize the American social arena. By the end of the year 2003, America had an average of 3.5 million millionaires. By the end of 2015, the number had risen to 10.4 million.

In 2016, Microsoft cofounder Bill Gates, the richest person in the world, was said to have a net worth of $75 billion. His net worth was considered greater than the GDP of 122 countries. The nature of the American marketplace makes that possible.[16]

The Technological Substructure

In the 1990s Alvin Toffler said that "the control of knowledge *is the crux of tomorrow's worldwide struggle for power.*"[17] Through technological advancements America has earned herself a central place in the marketplace of the control of knowledge. America is the world's leading superpower, and this is largely due to its place at the forefront of technological advancements.

America leads the world in commercial aviation, computer industry, as well as space aviation. They furnish the world's leading specialists in these fields and more. The war in Iraq in the early 2000s launched a level of technological advancement that no other country of the world was able to match at that time: cluster bombs, night vision goggles, Global Positioning Satellites, and much more. Obama's administration introduced the first use of armed drones in warfare. America continues to furnish warships the dimensions of which are unimaginable in many civilized nations.

Any random poll of American students will reveal that an average student in American classrooms comes from a home with at least two computers with internet connection; while a study in 2004 showed that only about 2 percent of the entire world population had a regular access to the internet the same year. The numbers have improved overall with 88.6 percent of the U.S. population connected to the internet compared to the world's 50.1 percent in 2016.[18]

Life in America is becoming more and more technology dependent, while many parts of the world are still playing catch-up in the technology game. The boost in America's world of technology has pushed commerce in America to a higher level as technology has practically destroyed geographical limitations: video conferences, mobile phones with internet connectivity, iPods, podcasting, Wi-Fi, Twitter, WhatsApp, Facebook, and many more are the order of the day.

Linguistic Structures

One of the nations whose formal language has undergone the most dynamic transformation in this century may be the United States. America's dominant language, English, has long departed from her British roots in terms of grammar, syntax, and even lexical structures. Significant variations now exist between the meaning of certain words and sentences when used by the British and when used by Americans. Spelling has changed, and new vocabularies that were not previously English have been incorporated. Americans speak a version of the English language that is exclusively American.

It is always funny to hear Americans accuse the British of speaking with an accent. The possibility of that irony validates the fact that American English has taken its own unique identity. Even within American societies, we notice slight regional variations that further illustrate the significance of language as a cultural construct. English language has become a major tool, which has spread American culture to many parts of the world. English-language studies are popular in many nations who want to do business with America, especially Asian countries.

Social Arrangement

Over the years the phrase "social institutions" has been used by sociologists to suggest many different things. One sociologist took the trouble to give it a concise definition. Part of the definition states that social institutions are "purposive, regulatory, and consequently primary cultural configurations, formed unconsciously and/or deliberately, to satisfy individual wants and social needs bound up with the efficient operation of any plurality of persons."[19] Within these social institutions, such things as family structure, political arrangements, and educational programs are included.

For this work, the term *social arrangement* is used instead of social institutions since the term "institution" has been seen as an abstraction rather than a perceived reality.[20] Social arrangement would, therefore, include family structures, housing, educational programs, and institutions and structures dealing with human welfare and co-existence.

The traditional American society was clearly identifiable as constituting communities of families. Homogeneity was a factor that pulled people together. Being a nation of immigrants, each immigrant population tended to settle in the same area to provide support and protection to their kind. Family was a man, his wife, and children. Schools were locally controlled, as they were initially the creation of the individual communities, not the government.

Certain elements of the social structures listed above remain a big part of American social identity today. Schools remain a community-based effort, despite the current attempts by the state and federal governments to regulate and supervise educational practices. The most powerful decision-making body in the school system remains the local school board, publicly elected by the people to run the schools.

Given the steady urbanization process and the end of legally protected institutional discrimination in America, the makeup of communities is changing as people are now free to live wherever they choose. Some smaller communities continue to resist this change by refusing housing to the "out-group" despite all kinds of federal and state laws that prohibit such practices. The structure of the family has also changed. American family is now a mosaic. Some are made up of mom, dad, and children, others by man and woman with no children, yet others by just mom and children or dad and children. It could also be grandparents and grandchildren, two moms and children, two dads and children, just to name a few.

With the increasing rise in urbanization, U.S. society has continued to become more and more individualistic. The individualism of the twenty-first century may be said to be significantly different from that of the twentieth century. In the previous centuries Americans cared about what neighbors would say and how the community would react to certain behaviors and lifestyles, but today's America seems to care less. As much as the lifestyle or behavior does not hurt anyone else, the individual feels it is his or her constitutional right to carry on with it even if the whole community frowns upon it. Such radical shifts have made gay and lesbian marriages, once practically unheard of, front-page news in twenty-first-century America. The American family structure has changed forever.

THE INTERACTIONS BETWEEN THE AMERICAN CULTURAL SYSTEMS

There is a dynamic interaction that takes place between the American cultural systems. These systems are so interrelated that any change in one area affects what goes on in the other structures. Figure 3.3 illustrates this interaction.

Let's start with the technological structures that we have mentioned earlier. The rapid advancement in American technology is only possible because of the kind of capitalist economic system obtainable in American society. American citizens and corporations know that they have a free-market economy. Whatever they invent is theirs, and the government cannot take it away from them.

The American government facilitates entrepreneurial spirit and invention as it happens to be about the largest market for American corporations with a defense budget which at one point was larger than the combined national budget of the next ten developed countries behind them[21] (the Iraqi war years). Much of this money is spent on defense technology, which is usually outsourced to American corporations like Boeing and Halliburton.

America is proud to produce men like Bill Gates, who has taken the world of technology to another level. Gates is willing to put all his energy and resources into technological advancements because he stands to benefit substantially from it. It has made him the wealthiest man on earth, wealthier than many poor countries of the world combined.[22] American technological advancements have also affected its linguistic structures. Certain vocabularies that were practically unknown twenty to thirty years ago are now everyday language; for example, internet, email, web page, Facebook, Twitter, Instagram, and more.

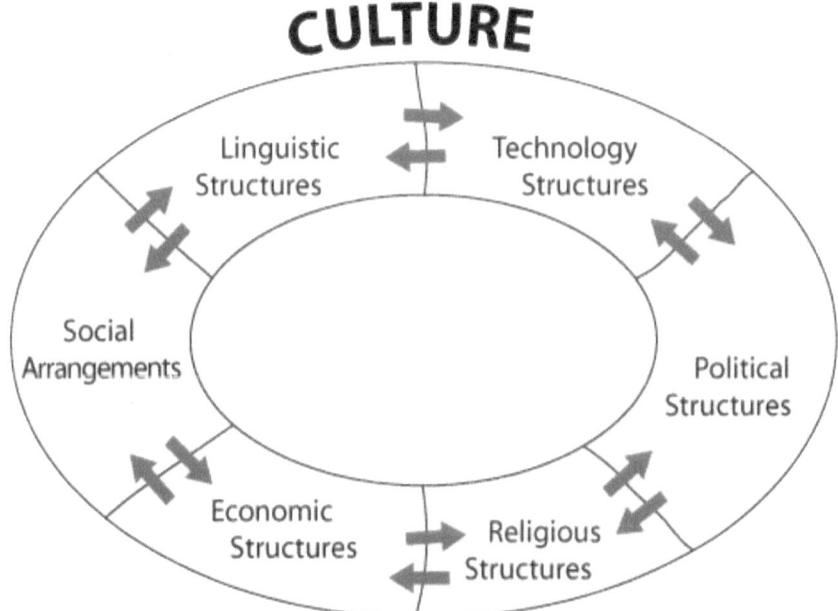

Figure 3.3. Interactions of Cultural Structures in the American Cultural Systems

The advancement in technology has its own ripple effects on the political landscape of America. In the 2004 elections, the Democratic primary elections felt the power of technology as Vermont governor Howard Dean used the internet to recruit a new breed of financiers for the Democratic Party that would have otherwise been ignored. With the power of the internet, he was thrown ahead of the other candidates for many weeks in the Democratic primaries. Barack Obama built upon this breakthrough in 2008, raising more money and support than any other politician before him; he became the first U.S. president of African descent, receiving more votes than any other past president in U.S. history.

In 2016, Donald Trump won the presidency using Twitter, fake news, and internet propaganda against Hillary Clinton. He is currently governing on Twitter, disregarding the conventional news outlets.

Electronic voting is another new addition to the American political landscape. With this system being developed in many states, reliability of election results is expected to be higher, and more people will also be able to vote. However, there is also a higher possibility for election fraud as computers can be programmed to swap votes. The U.S. government is currently investigating Russia's interference in the 2016 elections, which is suspected to have involved an attempt to hack into the electronic voting machines and rig the election in Trump's favor. Technology, therefore, can empower or disempower individual participation in the electoral process and consequently affect who is voted into office.

As the political structure is being affected, it is, on the other hand, affecting the social arrangement. In 2004 the mayor of San Francisco allowed city hall to perform gay marriages in violation of a state law that banned same-sex marriage. He was confident in doing this because, having surveyed his constituents, he believed he had enough support within his constituency to go ahead and do this. Politicians who feel that their constituents will side with a social agenda will work hard to push that agenda, even if it goes contrary to traditionally held views that had previously defined the American sociocultural landscape.

As politicians have empowered same-sex marriages through legislations and unilateral actions, traditional religious organizations are compelled to revise their positions on it. Denominations like the United Methodist Church, the Presbyterian Fellowship of America, and the Episcopal Church have all been fractured by elements that would take the politically correct position over and against the traditional stance of these churches.

With the recent U.S. Supreme Court ruling, gay marriage has become law in the United States. The social landscape is being redrawn as gay marriages take place and churches open their doors to them. It is not only the social and political movements that are reshaping America's religious landscapes; Russell Chandler (1995) identified such forces as immigration, ecology, education, media, and the arts, along with the other factors already identified, as forces that are reshaping America's religious landscapes.

THE AMERICAN WORLDVIEW AS THE CONDITIONING ELEMENTS OF CULTURE

Worldview is at the core of any cultural arrangement. Charles Kraft defined worldview as "the central systematization of conceptions underlying the way a people view reality." He described it as the factor to which the members of the culture (largely unconsciously) owe their conception of reality, "and from which stems their value system."[23] Worldview, therefore, is the hub that drives the wheels of culture. Figure 3.4 portrays the place of worldview in the cultural arrangement:

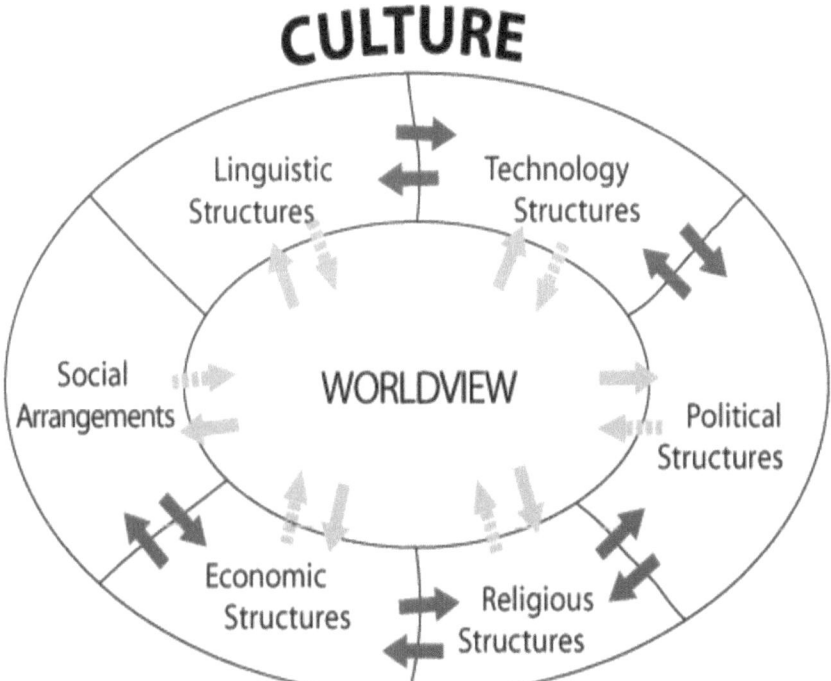

Figure 3.4. Worldview in Cultural Arrangements

First, in the diagram (figure 3.4), let's focus on the faint arrows going from the worldview into the different cultural structures. This illustrates how worldview quietly fashions these structures. The arrows are faint, suggesting the almost non-perceptive nature of the process by which worldview structures and forms the cultural systems.

To fully understand the nature of the American worldview, we must isolate each of the cultural structures we have already identified above, and discuss how worldview helped to shape them in the American cultural milieu.

American Worldview as the Conditioning Element of the American Social Structure

In the early definition of culture, we identified it as sets of ideas and belief systems. It is clear that ideas and belief systems are non-tangible elements. Ideas, particularly, originate from worldview. Even if we take Hidalgo's three levels of culture (1993), the place of worldview as the conditioning element of cultural structures is still central.

Values are one of the most visible elements of culture, yet these originate from the worldview level. Values cannot stand on their own without the concrete social structures that we call culture. Amitai Etzioni (1968) put it succinctly: "[V]alues not mediated through concrete social structures tend to become tenuous, frail, and, in the long run, insupportable."[24]

The idea of freedom led the first set of immigrants from Europe to leave their birth countries in search of a new life in the New World. This idea of freedom originated from their interpretation of the Bible, which asserts the sovereignty of individual lives and the right of humans to serve God by choice.

This idea of freedom influenced the way these immigrants lived their lives in the New World. Coupled with that idea of freedom was the idea of individual right to property ownership. Aware that they were not under any governmental restriction to reside in any one locale or practice a specific kind of trade, these immigrants wandered into the American hinterlands. A man, his wife, and children could go to the middle of nowhere, clear the bushes, erect a homestead, and establish a home. They were willing to fight off the natives alongside wild animals and other foes to establish themselves in a place of their own choosing.

This sense of freedom and individuality has now translated to a more observable social structure of single homes. Once they are of age, children are desirous to leave the home in search of their own future.

Unlike many other cultures, American parents are disinclined to pushing their children toward one profession or the other. They want the children to make their own choices, believing that this will help them stay happy. This is one way the worldview of a people helps shape their social organization. Another example is the fact that individual freedom and rights are at the heart of the restructuring that is taking place in the marriage institution in America today.

Many Americans do not like the homosexual lifestyle, but they recognize the rights of these individuals to live their lives the way they choose. The worldview that says they are free to make their choices and live their lives by their own standards is fundamental to the progressive thinking of today's America.

American Worldview: The Conditioning Element of the American Economy

At the heart of the American capitalist economic system is a Judeo-Christian Protestant ethic on money and material property ownership. This worldview, which traces back to the Anglo-Saxon Protestant origin of the mainstream culture, is the defining worldview that gives American capitalism its form. Max Weber was probably the first person to categorically link capitalism to Protestantism. According to him, capitalism, "as an economic system is a creation of the Reformation."[25]

Weber (1958) examined the writings of Benjamin Franklin, believing them to be influential in shaping American capitalism,[26] and thus he described American capitalism in very unique, yet culturally specific, language.

Weber saw American capitalism as the most naïve and open form yet to exist. His interpretation of Franklin yielded unique perceptions of capitalism. The reality of capitalism is presented in the following writings:

> In capitalist economies, the making of money takes on the character of a purpose rather than a necessity. It becomes a value rather than something that happens by chance or something that wells out of the avarice of a particular individual. There develops a collective "spirit" which advocates the idea that each person is called upon to make the utmost of his life and, furthermore, that the form this should take is devotion to industry in this world.[27]

The spirit of American freedom and individuality once again resonates in these statements. The individual is of a paramount significance, not the system. The worth of the individual, however, did not become as significant in relation to the system until, at least, the Reformation, when Luther advanced the place of the individual and his or her access to salvation by faith alone.[28]

As a result of the Reformation, the significance of the individual rose above that of the system. Cuzzort and King (1976), writing about Weber's discussion of American capitalism, stated, "Capitalism must be understood as a mass phenomenon. It is a culturally prescribed way of living; it is a complex of ideals; it is a change in the older moral order."[29]

Once again, the note of individualism resounds, a note that is very much a part of the American history and way of life. Some people would like to conceptualize the individual rights to property and individual freedom as "made in America." These are indeed fundamental human rights that America, more than any other nation on earth, helped push to the forefront of both political and economic ideologies. American capitalism, therefore, stems from America's view of life and reality—America's worldview.

The Judeo-Christian elements can be found in numerous Bible references that emphasize hard work and individual right to property. The Parable of the Workers in the Vineyard (Matthew 20:1–16) addresses the case of a landowner who hired laborers to work in his vineyard. He hired the first set in the morning, negotiated a wage with them and put them to work. At noon he hired another set and put them into the same field. Just an hour before the workday ended he hired yet another set of workers and put them in the same field.

The story goes on to state that at the end the vineyard owner pays the workers the same amount of wages. The earliest workers started to grumble and accuse him of unfairness. He asked them whether he paid them a penny less than their agreed wage, and they answered no. He then questioned why they would begrudge his generosity. He chose to use his money the way he pleased, and they had no reason to complain.

Another Bible parable talks about a master who gave his servants varying amounts of money as he was about to travel. To one he gave five talents, to another three, and yet another one. The first two traded with their talents and made profits of the same amount, thus doubling their talents. The last one chose not to invest the money, and quickly gave it back to the owner upon his return, claiming he was afraid of losing it. The owner scolded him and took the one he had and gave it to the one who had ten, thus making him richer (Matthew 25:14–30).

Here is another classic illustration of the benefit of hard work and industry as well as its accompanying benefit of keeping the whole profit, an underlying ideology of the American capitalist economy. The Judeo-Christian economic principles therefore are fundamental to the way Americans buy and sell.

American Worldview as the Conditioning Element for Our Technological Climate

Twenty-first-century America is the world's leader in the field of technology. Competition and the drive to be free is at the root of American technological advancement. America is always afraid of the emergence of another world superpower that can overthrow her democracy and rob her citizens of their freedom. The need to safeguard her freedom and democracy pushes America to invest invaluable resources and energy into technological advancements.

It is estimated that America's annual defense spending during the Iraqi war was larger than the annual military budget of the next twenty industrialized nations behind America, combined.[30] A significant portion of this budget goes into technology.

A more significant insight is that much of these technological advances start at individual nongovernmental corporate levels. Businesses and corporations develop these technologies and then they try to sell them to the government. In many other countries, individual corporations cannot even attempt developing these technologies without the government authorizing them to do so. But a country based on free-market economy and individual rights like the United States provides a context for such excursions into the world of the technologically unknown.

American Worldview as the Conditioning Element for Religious Plurality

America of the twenty-first century can be said to be religiously pluralistic. This is a statement many conservative Christians would rather not hear, but it is the reality of the American religious landscape. When in the First Amendment the founding fathers stated that "congress shall make no laws establishing religion or prohibiting the free exercise thereof," they entrenched in our national life and social structure, a pluralistic ideology as the defining element for the American religious landscape. It is possible that given the overwhelming Christian presence of that era, the full implications of this declaration were probably not evident, but as America matures and takes shape as a country of immigrants, the reality of the American pluralistic religious landscape has come into clearer focus.

An interpretation that has often been read into the religious freedom part of the First Amendment is that when this open door to religious expression was established, what was known as religion by most people in America at that time was in actuality differing expressions of Christianity, Judaism, and inconspicuous elements of fraternities and sects that may have some religious forms, like the Freemasons.

Robert Nisbet (1965),[31] in his interpretation of Emile Durkheim's views on religion, attributes to him an assertion that religion exerts limitless influence on culture and personality. The fundamental principle, however, is that the American founding fathers had a great regard for the sovereignty of an individual's right to choose how they would worship God. This understanding does not restrict this right to just Christians but to every individual expression of worship to God—or even a deliberate refusal to worship him. At the heart of this declaration is a fundamental evangelistic interpretation of the Christian faith.

The call to worship God, according to the New Testament, is a call to the individual. The Gospels give the individual a choice to respond one way or the other to the call to faith. The Gospels oppose the use of force in bringing anyone to faith in Jesus Christ. This understanding of worship is responsible for the Pilgrim's refusal to be restrained by the Church of England, hence the search for a land of freedom where they could exercise their faith without the intervention of government.

Freedom of worship, therefore, is fundamental to the American way of life. It is at the heart of the founding principles of this land, and remains a principle that sets America apart from most nations on earth. This is a unique cultural element, brought about by a very strong Evangelical Christian worldview.

THE INTERACTIVE NATURE OF CULTURAL STRUCTURES AND THEIR EFFECT ON WORLDVIEW

The American cultural structures, like that of any peoples' group, are not independent entities. They are codependent, and we have established that fact. A more significant factor, however, is that these structures also interact to produce significant shifts and changes at the core of the society's worldview patterns. Worldview, therefore, is not a constant. It is subject to modifications given a level of interaction with various cultural structures and societal forms. A significant change in one or more cultural structures can produce a major rearrangement of the worldview patterns, and significantly alter the worldview.

In the case of the American cultural arrangement, the sudden invasion of religious pluralism has led to a rearrangement of the way American societies are expressing their religious freedom. There was a time in America when the worldview was significantly religious, and that religious worldview was essentially Christian. Over the years, gains made during the civil rights movement empowered some individuals to openly begin to express a nontheistic worldview.

This movement has been further enhanced by advancements in the fields of science, as secular science gradually moves away from a religious explanation of the origin of life. An overtly religious explanation of divine intervention in life situations has practically given way to a more existential explanation in the American popular worldview. This is a major shift in conceptualization of reality.

Another area where changes in the cultural structures have rearranged our worldview is in the area of social arrangements. The classic American concept of family until recently has been husband and wife, with or without children. In recent years, along with increased divorce rates and the fact that liberal minds have pushed same-gender unions as civil rights, the family has been redefined. As society allows civil rights to take precedence over the preservation of *status quo*, the worldview on the definition of family has practically changed. It has become politically incorrect to see same-sex partnerships as indecent—a previously respected way of viewing same-sex unions.

A constant dynamic of this nature of worldview rearrangement is that it is usually a painful process. The worldview is the most resistant arena of change in any cultural arrangement. Any issue that attempts to alter the way a people view reality—marriage, family, religion, humanity—is usually strongly resisted. In figure 3.5, the arrows from the individual cultural structures to the worldview suggest that the dynamics of change and alteration are deliberately presented as faint and broken because it is never a straight shot due to the nature of the opposition that it encounters before it finally succeeds.

It is significant, therefore, to be aware of the fact that when we aim at altering any individual structure within a cultural arrangement, we are not only

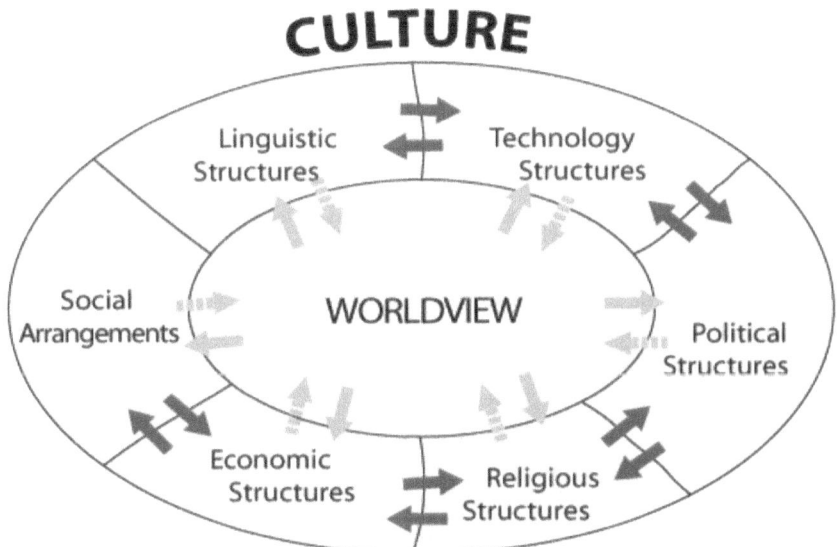

Figure 3.5. Worldview Alterations

changing that structure, but attempting to change the whole society's worldview. The broken arrows demonstrate how often the changes that take place in one simple cultural system can affect the whole worldview arrangement.

Recently in America, there has been a battle between the gay rights movements and groups and individuals who hold to a traditional view of family and marriage. For most people, when the gays and lesbians ask for rights to be married and to be recognized and accepted by society as legitimate unions, it is simply a matter of civil rights. For others it is more than that. It is a matter of worldview alteration. A recognition of gay marriage as legitimate affects the way society sees marriage and family for the endless future. Family trees will no longer be what we have traditionally known them to be. These changes will affect our tax systems, religious expressions and doctrines, marketing strategies, and even our political structures.

Another example of this worldview restructuring might be taking place outside the United States, as we speak. A few years ago, America undertook to overthrow Saddam Hussein's dictatorship and introduce democracy to Iraq. It sounded lofty and good, but the reality is that the introduction of democracy has affected all the other structures of Iraqi society: economy (free market), language (English will become more commonly used), religious (Christian religious and non-Christian religious faiths will find inroads), technological (capitalism opens the door to more contemporary technology), and social arrangement (the place of women and minorities will be redefined and improved).

As these structures are being revised, the way Iraqis view reality is changing forever. The emergence of groups like the Islamic State of Iraq and Syria (ISIS) represents a strong resistance to this cultural and worldview shift.

QUESTIONS AND APPLICATION

Case Study: The Cultural Rearrangement of Iraq

In April 2003, the United States government, under President George W. Bush, began a war to oust Iraqi dictator and human rights violator Saddam Hussein. Lots of speculations have taken place in an attempt to come to terms with the real motive for this war, but the official position is that Saddam Hussein's administration posed a threat to the security of the United States; it was suspected of ties with terrorists as well as being engaged in the production and possible use of weapons of mass destruction. Another compelling government position was that his records of human rights violations demanded an end to Saddam's rule of tyranny and the ushering in of a new era of freedom and human rights protection in the spirit of America's concept of democracy.

By implication, therefore, the U.S. government was not entering Iraq with the sole purpose of removing Saddam but with an added agenda of establishing a democratic political order in a country and region that have never experienced democracy.

CHALLENGE QUESTIONS

a. In view of the fact, therefore, that political arrangement is an essential part of a society's cultural structure, how would a foreign imposition of democracy into Iraq likely affect the culture and structure of the future Iraqi society?
b. Should the U.S. government succeed in imposing a democratic government, what other cultural structures and institutions of Iraq would be altered positively?
c. Should the U.S. government succeed in imposing a democratic government, what other cultural structures and institutions of Iraq would be altered negatively?
d. In what ways would a democratic government affect the worldview of Iraqis, which has been essentially egalitarian and theocratic?
e. Should the U.S. desire to establish democracy succeed, what factors are likely to provoke Iraqi resentment and opposition to the U.S. government?

ACTIVITY

Describe the unique cultural factors within the American way of life that distinguishes it from other democracies of the world. Compare U.S. capitalism to the capitalism of Great Britain.

STRATEGIES FOR APPLICATION

Many different activities can be used to apply lessons from this chapter to K–12 educational settings:

1. *Research Projects*: Grades 4–12 students can research their city, county, or state using U.S. census data to determine the ethnic distribution of people across their chosen locality. They can further investigate the history and immigration pattern of each group, finding out when they began

their immigration to the United States and why; how they have adjusted to U.S. culture over the years; what social, political, economic, and cultural challenges they have had to deal with over the years.

2. *Field Trips*: Teachers of K–12 students can organize field trips through historical sites in their city, county, or state. During such field trips, the history and cultural experiences of the various peoples of the city, county, or state will be the focus of investigation and discussion. Also, field trips to science and technology museums can be used as a way to help K–12 students engage the impact of technology and technological advancement on the culture of a people.

Chapter Four

Engaging the Crises of Cross-Cultural Encounters

> **Chapter Objectives:**
>
> The purpose of this chapter is to discuss the crises of cross-cultural encounters, bias, prejudice, and other factors that often result from variance in cultural values, as well as different levels of cultural values adjustment. Readers will be able to do the following:
>
> 1. Define cultural values and explain cultural values adjustment
> 2. Explain the implications of cultural values adjustment and maladjustment for multicultural education
> 3. Take a cultural values adjustment survey to determine the extent of their own cultural values adjustment

The need for multicultural education arises from the stress of cross-cultural encounters. Humans do not exist in isolated culturally homogeneous units anymore. We live in a global age, where barriers of race, ethnicity, distance, and civilization are continuously shrinking. How we relate to one another in this global age, however, is often determined by some beliefs and ideas that we hold about groups or individuals who are different from us. Prejudice and bias have remained major factors that have led to crisis in cross-cultural encounters. In this chapter we will attempt to explain how we develop cultural prejudices and biases, as well as attempt to propose practical ways to engage them.

The crises of cross-cultural encounters often focus on a Eurocentric presupposition of supremacy over the other cultures. According to Lee and Bhuyan (2013), western professionals in cross-cultural encounters are often

Figure 4.1. Issues in Discrimination

charged to get to know the non-western "other" as a means toward improving racial, cultural, or gender sensitivity. It fails, however, to facilitate cross-cultural harmony because these professionals often see the knowledge as a way to improve their efficiency in helping the "other" while still maintaining social control and sense of superiority.

So, quite often these well-intentioned professionals would be providing needed services while at the same time being discriminatory and racially biased against the very people they serve. Many classroom teachers in the American education setting fall prey to this when they come into the classroom with biased mind-sets.

CULTURAL VALUES ADJUSTMENT: A THEORETICAL BASIS FOR ENGAGING INTERETHNIC AND INTERCULTURAL ENCOUNTERS

In a study of the writings of Professor Jerzy Smolicz on Australian ethic cultural values, Secombe (2016) introduced the idea of intercultural space as cultural domain or social context in which people from different cultural groups interact, communicate, and meet. She explains that this context of intercultural interactions while physical and geographical, could also be virtual or intellectual. She confronts the need to avoid allowing one single cultural group dominance over intercultural spaces.

A factor that must be confronted in the twenty-first century is that intercultural spaces are becoming more and more normative rather than unique. A common problem that arises in intercultural spaces is dealing with prejudices and conflicts that arise from intercultural encounters.

Kent Koppelman and R. Lee Goodhart (2005) explained two different ways people attempt to explain prejudice: (1) the process of forming opinions without looking at relevant facts, and (2) being irrational.[1] In responding to the idea that prejudice is the process of forming an opinion without looking at relevant facts, they argue that often people with prejudice do examine relevant facts and simply interpret them to confirm their prejudices.

For the view that prejudice is irrational conclusions, they argue that rational people sometimes hold prejudices. They gave examples: (1) Aristotle, who claimed that women were inferior to men; (2) Abraham Lincoln, who held that African-American people were intellectually inferior to white people;[2] and (3) Martin Luther, the leader of the Protestant Movement, who told German Christians, "[D]o not doubt that next to the devil you have no enemy more cruel, more venomous and virulent, than a true Jew." Each one of these men was an icon in their various fields. They were critical thinkers, yet highly prejudiced individuals.

The question that arises from the realization that perfectly rational and well-meaning people can be highly prejudiced is this: Why? Koppelman and Goodhart (2005) attempted to suggest factors that lead to prejudice. Among those are elitism and zero-sum attitudes:

1. Elitism: This is the belief that most people succeed in society because they possess what it takes to succeed, while those who fail to succeed are naturally flawed and their failure to succeed is nobody's fault. This leads to a sense of entitlement and a condescending attitude toward others.
2. The Zero-Sum Attitude: The idea here is that sharing power is not in the best interest of the person in possession of power, since the assumption is that the personal gain of one individual means a loss to the other.[3]

Koppelman and Goodhart (2005) also mentioned the 1982 book by J. Levin and W. Levin in which they identified four causes of prejudice:

- Personal frustration: Personal failures and frustrations often lead the frustrated individuals to "scape-goating" tendencies.
- Uncertainty about the "out-group": Humans are usually afraid of the unknown. Avoidance exacerbates prejudices. Distance creates fear.
- Threat to one's self-esteem: U.S. society trains people to develop self-esteem by comparing themselves with others. People are encouraged to develop a superiority complex as a way of validating the self.
- Competition: Competition for scarce resources like jobs, good homes, even prestige and recognition, create grounds for putting down others so as to elevate the self.[4]

With due respect to these views and explanations, it needs to be argued that a fundamental factor responsible for the perpetuation of prejudice and intolerance is conflicts in cultural values. In order to make this argument, we must understand the meaning of values, cultural values, and the crises of cultural values adjustment.

Values

Values can be defined as sets of highly regarded codes of conduct and behavior parameters adopted by an individual, organization, or society. These codes guide one's behaviors, interactions, and judgments. Stephen Covey[5] defined values as "the worth or priority we place on people, things, ideas, or principles." Values are self-chosen beliefs and ideals; internal and subjective, based on how we see the world. Values are shaped by upbringing, society, and personal reflections.

Cultural Values

Janet Kalven (1982) asserts that human values are formed through the rewards and punishments that our parents, teachers, and peers mete out to us. Every child is born and raised within a cultural context. That context defines for the child what is good and bad, moral or immoral. This is what we call ethics. It also defines acceptable and unacceptable public and private behaviors, which often fall within the realm of etiquette. Beyond these two, however, the sociocultural context also defines the boundaries of social interactions.

It defines for the child who belongs and who does not belong within the social arrangement, which defines him or her. Factors such as ethnicity, race, socioeconomic status, religion, and so on, are the criteria used to determine who is within and who is outside of this social arrangement. This child grows up seeing the world exclusively from this perspective, believing that these arrangements are natural limits within which he or she must operate.

Secombe (2016) also referred to core values that are needed for meaningful exchange and coexistence in the intercultural space. She made reference to Znaniecki (1968), who alluded to shared human values that are somewhat universal, which underlie our social, psychological, and cultural existence on the planet earth.

Raths, Harmin, and Simon (1966) put this in a more technical frame when they identified seven traditional approaches to teaching values:

- Setting an Example: When parents and teachers model behaviors for their children or students.

- Rules and Regulations: Established to promote or discourage certain behaviors.
- Persuasion: Use of reasonable arguments to convince an individual to adopt certain values.
- Appeal to Conscience: Parents and teachers use this approach to discourage or dissuade a youngster from accepting or adopting an inappropriate or unacceptable value.
- Limited Choices: Parents and teachers manipulate behaviors by limiting choices children can make (e.g., Some American white parents have been known to tell their girls, "You are never to come home with an African American man to this house"). You limit the choices for them upfront.
- Inspiration: Values are reinforced or recommended through inspirational materials like speakers, books, films, music, etc.
- Dogma: We teach cultural or religious dogma, which prescribes certain values and discourages others. For example, "This is how our family has always done it" or "That is what the Bible says."[6]

Cultural Values Adjustment

The idea of cultural values adjustment assumes that no cultural system is perfect in and of itself. It also assumes that no cultural system exists in complete isolation. The fact of our imperfection and the necessity of social interaction with others demand that we adjust our worldviews and value systems to be more accommodating of people outside of our own cultural arrangements. Secombe (2016) refers to Smolicz's idea that the intercultural space demands modifications and adjustments to people's core and overarching values. The focus of this next section, then, is to address the nature of that adjustment.

The challenge of cultural values adjustment comes as a child is exposed to other cultural values and social factors outside of what he or she has been taught. These new cultural values and standards confront some children early in life, if they are privileged to go to school in a multicultural environment. By mere interaction with children from other sociocultural environments their cultural values are challenged, and if the school environment encourages diversity and social integration, they will begin to adjust their cultural values very early in life.

For kids who are raised in culturally sheltered environments like those in suburban America or some inner cities where the population is homogenous, children do not get this opportunity very early in life. The opportunity comes again if they have the chance to attend college in a culturally diverse environment. Most kids who are raised in the inner cities and happen to go to college are able to experience this shift during college years because the chances are high that they will attend a college with a diverse student population.

For some white kids from suburban America, however, a good number of them end up attending schools where most of the student population is from their own ethnic and socioeconomic levels. These students miss out, once again, on having their cultural values challenged, so they keep holding on to the views they learned in their suburban communities.

A few of these kids, however, who happen to attend college in ethnically and/or economically diverse contexts are confronted with new and different sets of cultural values, and they are challenged to adjust their previously held views in order to accommodate an expanded, and more inclusive, cultural value system. This challenge often comes from classes that are structured to engage these issues. Sometimes, however, they can come from students' personal interactions and encounters with people from different backgrounds.

If the pressure comes as a result of academic discourses, analyses and synthesis of social situations and issues of social justice/injustice, students are able to make personal decisions that can result in cultural values adjustment that enables them to be open, receptive, and accommodating of other cultures and worldviews. Depending on the nature of the academic discourse, some students shut down and refuse to open themselves up to any new cultural values that would differ from what they have brought from home.

This adjustment is most effective when it happens during interpersonal encounters. This may result from sharing a dormitory room with students from other sociocultural backgrounds, being on the same sports team, or being in a study group, fraternity, or sorority. As students get to know each other on a personal level, they are able to adjust their cultural values to accommodate their new friends and ensure that they get along.

The academic discourse in the classroom setting often serves to facilitate this but does not accomplish values adjustment single-handedly. The end product of cultural adjustment is individuals who have allowed their cultural values to expand to accommodate and include other cultures. In so doing they redefine for themselves a new cultural identity. They are no longer the individuals that left home to go to college; instead, they are new personalities with new (enhanced) values that are expanding beyond their childhood cultural boundaries.

This is the kind of experience that makes it possible for some kids who are raised in culturally shielded environments to still find themselves in interethnic or interracial marriages. They have grown to acquire a new appreciation of some cultures that are outside of their own cultural boundaries.

More significantly, individuals who have undergone this adjustment process are able to function more effectively in a culturally diverse environment.

Professionally they are able to work more collaboratively with individuals who are from different cultural backgrounds. If they are teachers, they are more capable of creating a diversity-sensitive learning environment in which all students feel affirmed and accepted.

Rosa Hernandez-Sheets (2009) described these teachers as culturally inclusive teachers.[7] They are culturally competent teachers who can facilitate learning for all children. Randy Lindsey et al. (1999, 2005)[8] refer to this level of competency as cultural proficiency. It is important to discuss factors that inhibit this level of competency or proficiency in individuals as we explore avenues to promote cultural competency, hence the discussion on cultural values maladjustment.

Cultural Values Maladjustment

Cultural values maladjustment is found in individuals who have either been deprived of the proper exposure to other cultural values or have refused to allow their own previously held cultural values to be challenged and adjusted. In the first instance, when individuals are raised in a culturally shielded environment, they do not possess the necessary skills and dispositions to see any credible value in cultural views and expressions outside of their own. This is not necessarily their fault; rather they have become victims of a myopic and conservative upbringing.

Some individuals live their entire lives at this level, avoiding everything that looks different from the values and cultural orientations that they have known all their lives. Those foreign elements threaten and create discomfort, so the human tendency is to avoid them.

On one side, this could be one of the factors responsible for the failure of some white public school teachers to embrace and promote diversity. At a personal level they have not adjusted their cultural value systems to accommodate new cultures, so they are unable to promote diversity.

On the other hand, it is the same reason why some minority students, especially African-American students from the inner cities are unable to function effectively in some American academic environments. They see academics as a foreign culture, a white culture. Given the fact that their own cultural value systems have not been adjusted to see and embrace the good in the white culture, they tend to reject everything white in its entirety. Students who try to embrace academic pursuit are seen as selling out to the white culture and consequently ostracized.

Those people who have deliberately refused to allow their cultural values to be revised or adjusted represent the other category of people who are victims of cultural maladjustment. These are individuals who have been exposed to the other cultures; they may have gone through diverse K–12 schools and taken college courses that promoted diversity, yet they resolved within themselves that their own cultural values are superior to all others and should be the only standard by which they live their lives and operate, even in professional environments. Such individuals would see courses in which their culture is critiqued as disrespectful and opposing to their culture, and they would take a defensive stance rather than critique their own culture despite insights from the course.

Such people can finish a whole course in cultural diversity and conclude that it was a complete waste of their time. They tend to see the world exclusively in terms of "We" versus "Them." Their cultural boundaries are immovable, almost cast in stone. In their private lives, they are those who refuse to walk across the street to get to know the neighbor who looks different. Society often brands such people as racists, but many of them do not fit that categorization. They do not want to cross their cultural boundaries to get to know you because it disturbs their cultural psyche, but they have no problems with your existence and opportunities.

These people are simply ethnocentric. The world as they know it is their cultural arrangement, and anything outside of it is foreign. In the United States, you will find people fitting this category among whites, African Americans, Hispanics, Asians, and other ethnicities. There might be a disparity in the distribution across ethnic groups, but they nevertheless exist across the board.

Implications of Cultural Values Maladjustment for Multicultural Education

In the United States, whereas laws have been enacted to enforce integration in American public schools, they have proved inadequate in establishing a cohesive society. Some state education boards in the United States have instituted mandatory diversity training for all teachers in an attempt to promote integration and cohesion, yet the success rate in cultural competency has not been significant. A fundamental factor responsible for this deficiency is the disproportion between the ethnic composition of the students that are taught and the teachers who teach them, especially in the inner cities.

White males and females represent more than 80 percent of the teacher population in America's K–12 classrooms.[9] A very high percentage of this teacher population is raised in shielded suburban environments, thereby implying their need for cultural values adjustment. Some of these teachers are willing to go and obtain the necessary training that would enable them to undergo this cultural values adjustment allowing them to function better in a progressively diverse school environment; some are closed to the idea and refuse to allow their cultural comfort zones to be invaded.

When the state of California instituted the Cross-cultural Language and Academic Development (CLAD)[10] certification for all teachers, they mandated all practicing teachers go back to school and get the certification or take an exam to waive the classes. Whereas some teachers immediately took advantage of the continuing education opportunity it offered, others who were nearing their retirement took early retirement or postponed it as long as they could and then retired. Still others decided to do nothing about it hoping it would all go away with time. Such people later found themselves trapped as the federal No Child Left Behind (NCLB) mandate added teeth to this requirement, and their jobs were threatened.

The big question is how one can expect teachers who are culturally maladjusted to teach multicultural student populations. This is basically what the educational system is doing today, and the proposition here is that we must first find ways to address this problem among teachers before we can expect them to teach multicultural populations. The section below provides a tool for measuring levels of personal cultural values adjustment. Follow the instruction and evaluate your level of personal cultural values adjustment.

CULTURAL VALUES ADJUSTMENT SURVEY

Please circle only one option ("a" to "e") for each question that best represents you.

1. Personal (unassigned) readings on other cultures and worldviews
   a. does not really appeal to me.
   b. is something I would love to do.
   c. is something I do on an ongoing basis.
   d. has contributed significantly to my knowledge base about the world and other cultures.
   e. significantly influences my lifestyle, professional practice, and social interactions with people from other backgrounds.
2. Sharing living space with somebody from a different ethnic background or race
   a. has never really appealed to me.
   b. is something I would love to do.
   c. is something I have done in an arranged setting like dormitory rooms.
   d. is something I have voluntarily undertaken once.
   e. is something I have done by choice on repeated cases.

3. Educating others on cultural diversity and its benefits
    a. is something I have never thought of doing.
    b. is something I would love to do if I had the skills.
    c. is something I have always desired to do given the skills I already possess.
    d. is something I have been able to do in a formal (work-related) setting.
    e. is something I do both formally and at a personal level.
4. Sensitivity to how I interact with people from other cultures and ethnicity
    a. is something I have not really given much thought to.
    b. is something I would love to be more conscious about.
    c. is something I am becoming more conscious about.
    d. is something that I have made part of the principles undergirding my social interactions.
    e. has enabled me to make friends across ethnic groups and sociocultural boundaries.
5. Rethinking my cultural value systems
    a. is something I have not really given much thought to.
    b. is something I would love to be more conscious about.
    c. is something I am becoming more conscious about.
    d. is something that I have made part of the principles undergirding my social interactions.
    e. has enabled me to make friends across ethnicities and sociocultural boundaries.
6. Consciously rearranging the way I look at other cultures and peoples
    a. is something I have not really given much thought to.
    b. is something I would love to be more conscious about.
    c. is something I am becoming more conscious about.
    d. is something that I have made part of the principles undergirding my social interactions.
    e. has enabled me to make friends across ethnicities and sociocultural boundaries.
7. Involvement in social action
    a. is something I have not really given much thought to.
    b. is something I would love to be more conscious about.
    c. is something I am becoming more conscious about.
    d. is something that I have made part of the principles undergirding my social interactions.
    e. has enabled me to make friends across ethnicities and sociocultural boundaries.
8. Establishing and maintaining friendship with people of a different cultural or ethnic origin from myself
    a. is something I have never thought of doing.
    b. is something I would love to do if I have the opportunity.

c. is something I have always desired to do given the opportunities I already have.
d. is something I have been able to do in formal (work-related) settings.
e. is something I do both formally and at a personal level.

9. Taking action to mediate in situations where people are discriminated against on racial or ethnic basis
    a. is something I have not really given much thought to.
    b. is something I would love to be more conscious about.
    c. is something I am becoming more conscious about.
    d. is something that I have made part of the principles undergirding my social interactions.
    e. has enabled me to make friends across ethnicities and sociocultural boundaries.

10. Choosing to abstain from racially or ethnically offensive jokes and discussions
    a. is something I have not really given much thought to.
    b. is something I would love to be more conscious about.
    c. is something I am becoming conscious about.
    d. is something that I have made part of the principles undergirding my social interactions.
    e. has enabled me to make friends across ethnicities and sociocultural boundaries.

Valuation for Response Key

The table below indicates the value of each response you picked in each question. Using this valuation key, tally the sum of your responses from questions 1 to 10.

Value allocation		
A	=	1:
B	=	2:
C	=	3:
D	=	4:
E	=	5:

Definition of Value Allocation

Each of the responses indicates levels of cultural values adjustment. The culminating value allocation gives you a general indication of where you are on cultural values adjustment. These levels are expected to change as you grow in cultural competency skills and abilities.

A = 1: Level one   – Adjustment deficiency
B = 2: Level two   – Openness
C = 3: Level three – Knowledge
D = 4: Level four – Respect and Appreciation
E = 5: Level five – Identification/Personal involvement and social action

Culminating Value Allocation

45–50 points – Highest level of cultural values adjustment. Well-adjusted and personally involved in fights for social justice and equality.
35–44 points – High level of cultural values adjustment. Characterized by diversity appreciation, relatively good sense of social justice, and possible social action.
25–34 points – Moderately adjusted. Open-minded and willing to learn about other cultures and worldviews. Making progress.
15–24 points – Slightly adjusted. Close-minded in certain areas but open in some others. Very slow progress. Needs more assistance.
10–14 points – Not well adjusted. Close-minded, resistant to change. Requires major paradigm shift.

THE EFFECTS OF WORLDVIEW IN THE DEVELOPMENT OF CROSS-CULTURAL IDEAS

Cultural values, ideas, and beliefs are not only developed in childhood, they are continually shaped and reshaped as we interact with social situations and issues around us. Worldview provides the basis for this ongoing development of ideas and belief systems. The development of ideas follows a pattern. The diagram in figure 4.2 illustrates the pattern.

Humans tend to recognize familiar patterns very quickly. These familiar patterns eventually develop into belief systems. Ideas and belief systems thus developed form the basis for our stories. These stories are the tools for justifying our perceptions. When our perceptions are wrong, it is difficult to see things differently because we have already developed a belief system that seems to be a logical by-product of our perception.

Culturally speaking, a good example of this process is the events of the terrorist acts on America that culminated in the destruction of the twin towers of New York City on September 11, 2001. A critical cross-cultural encounter took place as Americans watched those "foreigners" fly passenger jets into the twin towers. It was a very painful encounter that stimulated anger, fear, a sense of vulnerability, and bitterness toward Arabs and Muslims.

Engaging the Crises of Cross-Cultural Encounters 69

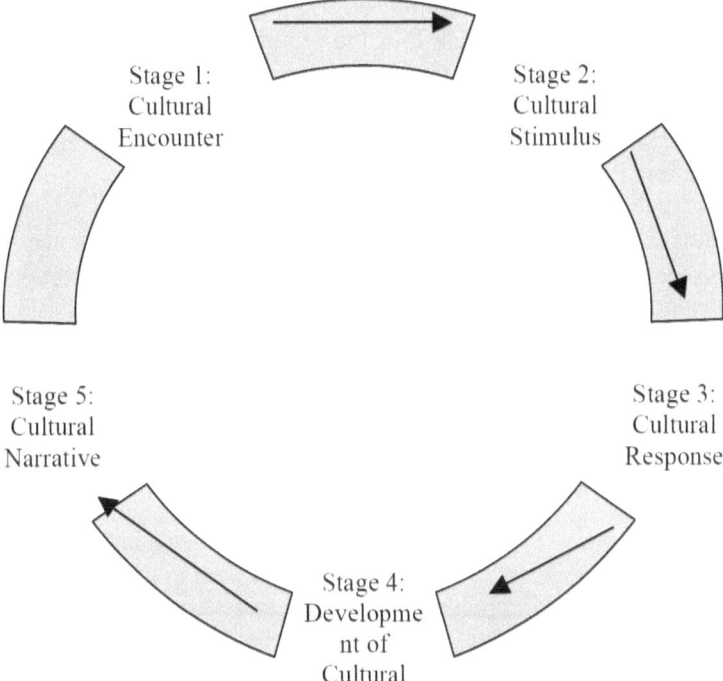

Figure 4.2. Development of Cross-Cultural Ideas

The responses in many parts of the United States were quick and sometimes deadly. It practically became a crime, and a capital crime in some parts, to travel or move around "while looking Arab or Muslim." Hate crimes were carried out against these people.

Many Americans became uncomfortable as soon as anyone dressed as a Muslim or Arab came by. The government tightened safety measures to fend off future attacks. Under the Patriot Act, people were delayed and sometimes detained without any charges. A more overwhelming cultural response was evident as American flags were displayed from home to home. Cars, too, were decked with various symbols of patriotism. Placards displayed all kinds of patriotic slogans. Young men volunteered for military service in order to go and get the enemy.

A cultural perception of distrust and unease with Arab Muslims soon became a part of the American public mind-set, to the extent that the credibility of long-term allies like Saudi Arabia was questioned. This has led to a major shift in America's worldview.

Whereas many people consciously tried to isolate the terrorists from the rest of the Arabs, the reality was that many more Americans became intolerant of

Arab Muslims. Even Malaysians, Indians, and Pakistanis, often mistaken for Arabs, suffered from the backlash of the hatred and resentment. Individuals who carried out these acts of hatred and intolerance felt justified to do so based on a cultural narrative that said, "Arab Muslims hate Americans, whether Saudis or Palestinians, they hate us. We cannot regard them as friends or allies. We must not allow ourselves to be deceived into trusting them."

This narrative is justified because of the series of terrorist acts against America by Arab Muslim terrorists, which culminated in the events of September 11, 2001. If this line of thinking is left unchallenged, it can become an entrenched cross-cultural belief system in the United States. The propensity for this requires us to evaluate the way we see cultures and different kinds of people over time.

CULTURAL AND PERSONAL BIASES IN THE EDUCATIONAL SETTINGS

A primary inhibition to students' academic performance and social development in schools comes from biases that are evident in the classrooms and the general school environments. Biases have a variety of root causes. Some of the causative factors include prejudice, stereotyping, ethnocentrism, and a number of other factors. Let's explore these root causes of bias in the schools and investigate the outward manifestations of bias in the educational setting.

Factors Responsible for Educational Biases

Prejudice may be the root cause of educational bias; but before we discuss prejudice, let's first define bias. Bias has been defined as "any attitude, belief, or feeling that results in, and helps justify, unfair treatment of an individual because of his or her identity."[11] A dictionary definition of prejudice, on the other hand, says it is hatred or disrespect based on an inflexible generalization about a given people or an individual.

Prejudice takes different forms. It could be exhibited in excessive pride in one's ethnic heritage, country, or culture, to the point that others outside that group tend to respond negatively to that group. In certain cases, prejudice is based on fear of the unknown, fear of contamination, and the negative human tendency to separate rather than unite. The fundamental problem in combating prejudice and racism is that they are not based on logical or rational conclusions; they are beliefs that have become stories, based on perceived conclusions that were not subjected to any rational logical critique.

Prejudice in the educational setting manifests itself in the form of racism, sexism, and other negative attitudes. Students often get punished excessively because of their cultural or social identity rather than for their immediate behaviors. This happens when certain behaviors that would be overlooked in a child from the dominant culture would be picked upon in a minority child.

Lots of studies have focused recently on how much minority students get punished for certain behaviors compared to students from the dominant culture. Studies are done on how boys are treated in the classroom compared to girls. One study reported that boys receive between five and ten times more disciplinary actions than girls do at the elementary and middle-school level. The same study points out that nearly two-thirds of the students in special education programs in the United States are boys.[12] Each one of these and related studies tend to reveal a new and troubling element in the educational system.

The number of minority children in special education classes continues to rise while the white students continue to dominate the gifted and talented programs. These tendencies have often been criticized as prejudicial and unfair.

Prejudice, therefore, manifests itself every time a child is not looked at, treated, or interacted with on the basis of his or her personal merit and demerit, but instead on the basis of group or ethnic expectations and categorizations. Such treatments undermine the rights of that individual child to fair treatment and quality education, and it undermines the fundamental principles of this country's laws and Constitution. It is illegal, it is immoral, it is wrong. Research has repeatedly shown that a teacher's effectiveness in promoting student achievement is intrinsically connected to that teacher's "deep-seated" beliefs and assumptions about the students, their character, potential, and intelligence.[13]

Being a teacher educator, this writer has the special privilege of going from one classroom to another, supervising and encouraging new teachers on the path to professional growth. One of the assignments I require my student teachers to do during student teaching is to write journals. They are required to write down special experiences and encounters that make their days challenging or rewarding. They are to take special notice of what goes on in the classroom and report back to me how they feel about the experience.

One student wrote about the master teacher's attitude to the different category of students. First he described the two classes of students:

> [T]he two classes I deal with, one "normal" and the other "gate" demonstrate a basic dilemma in terms of ethno-class stratification. This is more marked because for the most part average IQ and native mental abilities between the two groups appear to be unremarkably similar and probably just above average.... The difference between the two groups appear to me as motivational, self-ego, with continuous social reinforcement, greater involvement, interest and enrichment by parents, fundamental differences in social values and ethos between predominantly Chinese American and Mexican America patterns of enculturation and socialization, and especially perhaps the different ways the two groups are treated by the master teacher.

One may want to question the basis on which this student teacher can make assumptions about these students' backgrounds and IQs, as well as his basis for delineating the basic difference between the two groups to essentially environmental and social factors rather than genetic. It is important to note that this is not a regular student teacher. This teacher candidate already held a doctorate in cultural anthropology and was a seasoned researcher who had come into the field of education as a second career. He had the credentials, the skills, and the knowledge base to make the assumptions and judgments he made.

He wrote on the master teacher's expectations, attitudes, and treatment of these groups of students:

> Though they run on parallel schedules, in terms of their curriculum, it is clear that much more is expected from, and hence received from, the Gate group compared to the other, while the other tends to be scolded, admonished, and shouted at far more frequently for transgressions that are minor and similar in kind and frequency for both groups. I do not think the teacher realizes she is doing this[;] . . . she tends to try out new lessons on the "normal" class before modifying them to fit the Gate class. Both groups appear to have similar kinds of questions and problems with math work, and the rates and amount of information retention between the groups appears to be similar, though I would say because the Gate group tends to get greater and perhaps more consistent reinforcement in the home and in other extracurricular contexts, they tend to revisit and retain a greater amount than the other group.

Does this master teacher know what she is doing? How can she possibly claim to not know? She must know, but she may not know that it is unfair. She may not admit the bias that is so evident and entrenched. Anti-bias does not invalidate the need for differentiated curriculum. It calls for equitable and quality education for all. Anti-bias requires teachers to see the potential in every child and seek ways to harness it.

Teacher expectations have significant impact on how students achieve. A study done by Ladson-Billings[14] revealed that African-American students are more sensitive to the perceptions of their teachers than the white students, and consequently act to meet the teacher expectations. The implication of this is that if the teacher's expectations are low, the students will act accordingly; and if the expectations are high, they will act accordingly. Teachers must be willing to dispel the tendency to place low expectations on students because of ethnicity or disability.

FORMS OF BIAS IN THE EDUCATIONAL SETTING

Teacher/Administrator's Attitudes and Language

Teachers and the administrative staff all have a stand on issues of race, equity, and social justice. Such a stance is seldom spoken, yet very much pronounced. The way a teacher relates to students who are different from him or her ethnically, racially, or otherwise says something to other students in his or her classroom about how that teacher perceives ethnic or racial differences.

Teachers and administrators often come down very hard on minority students for offenses and infractions they would otherwise have glossed over had it been committed by students from the mainstream culture. When that happens, the minority students see themselves as scapegoats, and they become resentful of the system. Students from the mainstream culture often take advantage of that to lure these minority students into trouble, knowing that they are the ones most likely to get punished.

Some teachers and administrators adopt the color-blind approach. They choose to dismiss issues of ethnic and racial differences and try to treat every student the same. As much as this is well intended, the crises faced by the minority students are often overlooked, and their unique needs go unmet. Kids from poor homes or single-parent homes will struggle academically because of their unique situations. When we adopt a color-blind approach, we often overlook other underlying social factors that have nothing to do with ethnicity but which may hamper a student's academic progress.

Counselors' Attitudes and Language

Junior high and high school counselors may be the most influential people in students' journey to academic success. These counselors advise them on course selections and control the tracks they fall into. Sadly, some counselors categorize students based on their skin color or ethnic origin long before they even open their files to look at their academic abilities and other issues.

A college counselor told a young African-American girl, who had recently graduated from a University of California system, that the university was not for her type. He advised her to go to California State University at Dominguez Hills, because that's the school that is meant for her type. This straight-A student was a fighter who knew what she wanted in life, so she kept pushing until her admission to the same institution was granted. Four years later, that same woman was admitted to the same university's medical school.[15]

Many counselors inhibit the chances of minority students rather than enhance them by tracking them to particular schools or study programs. This is a persistent problem in the American education system.

Classroom Environments

Teachers need to pay special attention to how they arrange their classrooms. What cultural artifacts are displayed in their classroom? Do they represent the dominant culture, or are they inclusive? Where a student who looks different is seated makes a statement about how the teacher views his or her differences.

Students' Attitudes to One Another (the Hegemony vs. Minorities)

School culture often perpetuates divisiveness among students. Ethnic rivalry in schools often speaks to the general school climate. If the school climate is such that there is empowerment, cooperation, and collaboration, ethnic rivalry will be minimized. When white and African-American or Hispanic students begin to fight against each other purely across racial lines, it suggests that something is wrong with that school's culture and climate.

Students' attitudes toward one another can be improved if the administration is willing to invest in the development of an inclusive community. Simple steps toward this inclusion can be a collective celebration of ethnic holidays and events. Hispanic and African-American students have no reason to fight each other if they realize that they are both minorities and dealing with similar issues. When the school climate suggests to one group, no matter how subtly it is done, that they are better than the other, a seed of discord is sown.

OTHER ISSUES IN CROSS-CULTURAL ENCOUNTERS IN AMERICA

In this section we will briefly address a number of concepts and issues that multicultural educators must familiarize themselves with in the process of teaching in diverse learning environments. Our understanding of these issues and concepts as well as our attitudes to facilitating or discouraging them have significant implications on how well we do in fostering cross-cultural harmony.

Enculturation

Enculturation is the process of inculcating into an individual a given set of ideas, belief systems, worldviews, practices, and artifacts of a given culture or a social group. This can be simply defined as the process of culture acquisition. The way we raise children in our families is an enculturation process. English-as-a-second-language (ESOL) classes as well as the many institutes for American language and culture across college campuses are all enculturation processes and programs. The goal is to enable recent immigrants to fit into the new society and function more effectively.

Assimilation

This is the process by which individuals adopt the "behaviors, values, beliefs, and lifestyle of the dominant culture."[16] Under assimilation, the individuals lose their own culture completely and adopt the culture of the dominant group. In the American history of cultural interactions, the "assimilationist" ideology characterized the time between the turn of the twentieth century and World War I, culminating in the New Deal–era of post–World War II America.

This was the time when the Anglo-Saxon Protestant culture emerged as the dominant U.S. culture. The ideal was the melting pot whereby the immigrant population was required to give up all their ethnic characteristics and adopt the dominant culture. Two goals characterized the educational institutions of the time, namely, to rid ethnic groups of their ethnic traits and to force them to acquire Anglo-Saxon values and behaviors. Suburbanization of America sealed that movement.

One of the leading educational minds at the turn of the twentieth century, Ellwood Patterson Cubberly, stated the major goal of the common school:[17]

> "Our task is to break up these groups or settlements, to assimilate and amalgamate these people as part of our American race, and to implant in their children, as far as can be done, the Anglo-Saxon conception of righteousness, law and order, and popular government, and to awaken in them a reverence for our democratic institutions and for those things in our national life which we as a people hold to be of abiding worth."

The assimilation perspective is the same as the "melting pot" ideology. The fact that such thoughts and ideologies expressed above characterized individuals who have influenced the American educational system makes it more than imperative that we engage in a conscientious effort of redefining the goals of our educational structures in the twenty-first century, thus making multicultural education an indispensable aspect of our school curriculum.

Acculturation

This is the process by which individuals adopt the culture of the mainstream without necessarily giving up their own cultures. This was characteristic of the many early Eastern, Southern, and Central European peoples who came to the United States. Whereas they learned the English language, and the Anglo-Saxon ethics and etiquette, they maintained their cultures as they lived in their own communities and built their own churches and schools.

The possibility of retaining ethnic cultures while claiming to be American tends to pose a threat to some Americans who think that the ideal American image is the melting pot. These people fail to realize that the melting pot metaphor is just that—a metaphor; although the melting pot of the nineteenth and twentieth centuries accepted Europeans of every stock, it rejected Africans, Native Americans, Chinese, and Hispanics, until the civil rights movement compelled America to accept the fact that those people were also Americans.

America has been more of a salad bowl where the lettuce, the tomatoes, the cabbage, the carrots, and the celery all retained their individual identities, but were willing to be part of one meal, which is blended into an edible unit by a liquid called salad dressing. When eaten as one unit, the individual tastes combine to make the meal worth eating. That is indeed the reality of American ethnic diversity.

Accommodation

This is a two-way process by which members of the mainstream culture adapt to certain changes that come about as a result of the presence of a minority culture while the minority culture also adjusts some of its ways in the light of the dominant culture. The language of accommodation is often used loosely to suggest that the dominant culture is giving the immigrant culture an opportunity to thrive. It is often used to suggest that this is a favor being done for the minority culture for which they should be grateful.

In the context of schooling, however, every child has an equal right to be in school and to learn, and no child should ever be treated as though he or she is being "done a favor" by being allowed into the school and given an opportunity to succeed. Equal and quality education is a debt we owe all America's children regardless of race, ethnicity, socioeconomic status, and gender.

Accommodation must be seen as a symbiotic relationship in which the various cultural expressions that constitute the United States accept the validity of each cultural group, their right to be, and the need for them to advance themselves and then commit to making it happen. We must see ourselves as codependent groups who need one another to become the best we are capable of becoming.

Cultural Pluralism

This has been defined as a situation in which "members of diverse cultural groups have equal opportunities for success . . . in which cultural similarities and differences are valued, and in which students are provided cultural alternatives."[18] The America into which the earlier Western European immigrants and later the Eastern, Central, and Southern European immigrants lived together was not an assimilated America but a pluralistic America. The mere presence of these later European "peoples" threatened the earlier West European immigrants.

In 1917 and 1924 immigration acts were passed to limit the immigration of these non–Western Europeans to the United States. The effect of pure pluralism is ultimately seen in coexistences, intercultural (racial) marriages, integrated neighborhoods, integrated workplaces, and other avenues. These constitute the true vision of the American maxim, *E pluribus Unum*—out of many, one.[19]

Biculturalism

Biculturalism is the situation in which an individual is able to function effectively in two cultures. It is the God-given ability of the human species to function effectively under more than one platform. Some ladies are teachers, mothers, and wives as well. Some people like mashed potatoes with gravy on a turkey dinner and also love sushi. This is a simplistic example of what it means to be bicultural.

An example of biculturalism can be found in African-American, Japanese-American, and Mexican-American citizens. These are individuals who have had to deal with two different cultural heritages while still maintaining their individual identities. Biculturalism often comes with a price. Such a price was paid by Japanese Americans who were actively engaged in fighting America's enemies during World War II, while their families at home in America were being displaced and sent to internment camps.

Many of America's minority children in the public and private schools are bicultural. They are as American as can be. The culture into which they are born and are being raised is essentially American, yet many of them are still affected by the cultures of their immigrant parents and grandparents. These children often see themselves first and foremost as Americans, before any ethnic label. It is society that often tells them that they are not American enough because their physical features resemble those of their Asian, Hispanic, or African parents.

A Nigerian missionary once visited a Los Angeles classroom where his friend was teaching. As he was interacting with some of the students in the class who were of Asian descent, he asked one of the girls, "Where do you come from?" The student looked at him in wonder and asked, "What do you mean?" He struggled to explain himself. Evidently he wanted to know whether she was of Japanese or Vietnamese or Chinese descent. The student, however, did not like the question or its tone, but simply responded, "I am an American."

Our schools are full of bicultural students who are patriotic Americans, yet we have curriculum, policies, and procedures, as well as teachers (through conduct and words), that continually inform these students that they are foreigners in their own land of birth. The contemporary multicultural education goal is to remove these negative signals from reaching our students. We need to allow America's children to be the Americans they desire and are proud to be. The schools must help students realize that eating *sushi* or *dim sum* for breakfast instead of scrambled eggs and bacon does not make them any less American.

Racism

Racism can be defined as the assumption that certain traits possessed by one group of people distinguish them from others, making them either superior or inferior to others. Racism or racialism has been defined as a way of cognitively organizing perceptions of people around the world by certain immutable characteristics.[20]

The problem with this definition is that these so-called immutable characteristics remain vague and hard to define. Kevin Cokley (2002) identified some of these immutable characteristics to include behavior, intellect, and temperament.[21] These characteristics have been argued and debated in academic and political circles. The debates have influenced policies on the use of IQ tests on minority students, given the fact that the whole assertion that intellectual and behavioral differences can be seen as immutable racial characteristics has not been scientifically proven.

Skin pigmentation, more than any other characteristic, has been used as a defining physical factor that distinguishes the African Americans from the whites. Yet what is called African American or white has different shades and tones of skin color. Physical features have been used, in addition to skin color, to distinguish Asians from whites.

The fact remains, therefore, that the basic immutable racial characteristics that distinguish one race from another would vary when one race is compared to another, thereby invalidating its immutability. So, what has been characterized as immutable in one context may actually move and be replaced by another feature or characteristic in another context. In light of this possibility, the only thing that may have remained immutable in racial categorizations is the assumption of one race that they are superior to others.[22] That, on its own, is a faulty proposition.

Discrimination

Discrimination refers to unfair treatment of one person or group of persons because of prejudice about race, ethnicity, age, religion, or gender.[23] These actions limit the social, political, or economic opportunities of a particular person or group.

Openly segregated schools served as a form of institutional discrimination, but today it has been replaced by other forms of latent discrimination, which are seen in curriculum content, school financing, and quality of teachers, facilities, and so on. This is the focus of Jonathan Kozol in his *Savage Inequalities: Children in American's Schools* (1991).[24]

Ethnocentrism

Ethnocentrism is the cultural tendency of individuals or a peoples' groups to perceive reality exclusively from one's personal or cultural point of view. Other cultures and practices are judged by the standards of one's own culture and often despised and looked upon as inferior. My culture becomes the standard by which every other culture is judged. My own cultural etiquette becomes binding on others who may not necessarily value it. This perception limits a person's ability to engage people outside of his or her cultural experience in a respectful and effective manner.

QUESTIONS AND APPLICATION

Case Study: Handling Racial Slurs among Students

Background

You are a white female fourth-grade teacher in a suburban school with about 80 percent white students, 10 percent Hispanic students, 8 percent Asian, and 2 percent African American. Your class has no African-American student in it. Mr. Becks, a fellow fourth-grade teacher is an African-American man. He has one African-American student in his classroom. Mr. Becks is your team-teacher. You work together on a number of projects, including physical education (PE).

The Problem

One day during PE, Stanley, the one African-American student in Mr. Becks's class, comes to you to complain that Andrew, a white student in your class, used the "N" word on him. Andrew's parents are known racists. They believe in the superiority of the white race, and they have often said openly that they could use whatever racial slur they choose to use; it is their civil right.

THE CHALLENGE

a. What will you say to Stanley in response to the complaint he lodged with you?
b. How would you address Andrew on this matter? What will you tell him? What would you require him to do to placate Stanley?
c. Would you involve the rest of your students in this matter? Why? Why not?
d. Would you involve Mr. Becks in this matter? If yes, what would you want him to do?
e. Would you involve Andrew's parents in this matter? What would you expect them to do? Why would you choose to involve them or not to involve them?
f. What possible volatile issues must be avoided in handling this matter?

ACTIVITY

The United States of America reached a significant landmark in 2008 when Barack Obama was elected the first African-American president of the United States. Discuss the level of racism and prejudice against blacks in the United States today. Identify the different ways racism, prejudice, and bias against blacks and Hispanics still happen in the school systems using journal and newspaper resources. Discuss what you can do as a K–12 teacher to mitigate these for your black and Hispanic students.

STRATEGIES FOR APPLICATION IN THE K–12 CLASSROOMS

1. *Grades K–6*: Read the story of Ruby Bridges. Ask students to write personal journals on discrimination. Journals should focus on personal expe-

riences or things they have read or heard about. Journals should be posted on a bulletin board accessible to the whole school community.

2. *Grades K–12*: Ask students to reflect on the circle of their friendship and determine how many friends they have outside of their ethic/cultural circles. Encourage them to spend the week identifying someone from a different ethnic or cultural background and try and befriend that individual. Allow students to share their experiences openly at the end of the week.

Chapter Five

Educational Inequalities in American Schools

Chapter Objectives:

The goal of this chapter is to discuss the constitutional and legal basis for the struggle for educational equality in the United States of America. At the end of this chapter readers will be able to do the following:

1. Discuss the constitutional basis for the struggle for equal educational opportunities in the United States
2. Name and discuss the various landmark legal rulings on which the struggle for equal educational opportunities is anchored in the United States
3. Identify and discuss the various areas where the struggle for equal educational opportunity continues

---

WHAT IS EDUCATIONAL INEQUALITY?

James Banks, in an attempt to define multicultural education, stated that "[m]ulticultural education incorporates the idea that all students—regardless of their gender and social class and their ethnic, racial, or cultural characteristics—should have an equal opportunity to learn."[1] The question that arises from this concept of multicultural education is this: What does an equal educational opportunity really mean? How can we define equity to make sure that there is no ambiguity about it?

To understand what is meant by equity in the educational system, we will need to review some cases in American educational history that have anchored on the struggle for equality. These landmark cases were brought by groups and individuals who felt that their rights to fair and equal educational opportunities were being deprived them.[2]

Plessy v. Ferguson—Separate but Equal Doctrine

One of the foremost judicial rulings that set the stage for the unending battle for equality in America is *Plessy v. Ferguson*.[3] Critics have argued that prior to this ruling in 1896, the gap between the races was not as wide as this ruling drove it in the years that followed. During the Reconstruction era, the Southern states of the United States had adopted the Jim Crow laws requiring separate facilities (toilets, water fountains, recreational facilities, seating in public transportation and other places) for whites and colored Americans.[4]

The U.S. Civil Rights Act of 1875 promised common civil rights to all Americans.[5] An 1878 U.S. Supreme Court ruling indicated that states could not prohibit segregation on common carriers such as railroads, streetcars, or steamboats. In 1890, the General Assembly of the State of Louisiana passed a law providing for separate railway carriages for the white and colored races.[6]

The petitioner in *Plessy v. Ferguson* was a U.S. citizen residing in the state of Louisiana; he was of mixed blood in the proportion of seven-eighths white and one-eighth African blood. He argued that the colored blood was virtually indiscernible in him and that he was entitled to every recognition and privilege as was entitled to other white U.S. citizens. He had paid for a first-class ticket on the East Louisiana Railway from New Orleans to Covington. He entered the train and took a sit in the section where the white passengers were seated (the seat he paid for). With no previous law authorizing the trains to segregate the passengers on the grounds of race, the conductor required him to vacate the seat or face ejection from the train as well as possible imprisonment.

He refused to comply, and with the aid of police officers, he was ejected from the train and thrown into jail. In filing this case, the plaintiff argued that the state of Louisiana's segregation law violated the Thirteenth and Fourteenth Amendments, laws prohibiting slavery and prohibiting the states from restricting the rights of freed slaves.[7]

In delivering the U.S. Supreme Court ruling on this case, Mr. Justice Brown read the following:

> [W]e cannot say that a law which authorizes or even requires the separation of the two races in public conveyances is unreasonable, or more obnoxious to the Fourteenth Amendment than the acts of Congress requiring separate schools for colored children in the District of Columbia, the constitutionality of which does not seem to have been questioned, or the corresponding acts of state legislatures. We consider the underlying fallacy of the plaintiff's argument to consist in the assumption that the enforced separation of the two races stamps the colored race

with a badge of inferiority. If it is so, it is not by reason of anything found in the act, but solely because the colored race chooses to put that construction upon it.[8]

In this ruling, the courts accused the U.S. Congress of initiating the very first act of institutional segregation as they chose to approve the segregation of white and colored students in the District of Columbia, where they lived and worked. The ruling upheld a law that compelled under penalties the separation of two races in every form of public and social life. Based on this precedence and the judicial provisions of the Supreme Court ruling of 1878, the state of Louisiana had a solid basis for enacting their own law, which in this ruling the U.S. Supreme court upheld. This was the official ground upon which American schools were segregated for the next seven to eight decades.

Dissenting on this ruling, Justice Harlan, a member of the US. Supreme Court, stated as follows:

> The Caucasian race deems itself to be the dominant race in this country. And so it is, in prestige, in achievements, in education, in wealth and in power. So, I doubt not, it will continue to be for all time, if it remains true to its great heritage and holds fast to the principles of constitutional liberty. But in view of the Constitution, in the eye of the law, there is in this country no superior, dominant, ruling class of citizens. There is no caste here. Our constitution is color-blind, and neither knows nor tolerates classes among citizens. In respect of civil rights, all citizens are equal before the law. The humblest is the peer of the most powerful. The law regards man as man, and takes no account of his surroundings or of his color when his civil rights as guaranteed by the Supreme law of the land are involved. . . . In my opinion, the judgment this day rendered will, in time, prove to be quite as pernicious as the decision made by this tribunal in the Dred Scott case.[9]

What this case represents to us as we study the topic of social and educational inequality in America's public schools is the fact that our history has indelible records of social and educational inequalities that have been institutionally devised and implemented, and if left unchallenged continues on today. We live in a society where the concept of equality is not a generally agreed-upon term. Some citizens believe that equality does not mean they are equal with certain sections of the populace, and the governments and the legal institutions have often taken sides with such persons to ensure inequality in the historic past.

Brown v. Board of Education of Topeka, 347 U.S. 483

This 1954 court ruling is regarded as the final blow on the Separate but Equal doctrine of *Plessy v. Ferguson*.[10] The major contention in *Brown v. Board of*

Education of Topeka was that segregated schools are not equal, neither can they be made equal, and that they deprive the colored children their rights under the law. The Reverend Oliver Brown of Topeka, Kansas, had a little eight-year-old girl named Linda. Linda was forced, because of her race, to travel long distances to attend Monroe Elementary School (an all African-American school) when close to her home was Sumner Elementary School, an all-white school.

With the support of the National Association for the Advancement of Colored People (NAACP), Reverend Brown attempted to enroll his daughter in the neighborhood school by fall of 1950. She was denied admission, and on behalf of this family and thirteen other families, the NAACP filed a lawsuit against the board of education by February of 1951, which eventually reached the U.S. Supreme Court.[11]

The plaintiffs argued that the Separate but Equal doctrine of *Plessy v. Ferguson*[12] has no place in the educational setting. The plaintiffs, through their attorneys, sought the aid of the courts to gain admission into public schools in their communities on a non-segregation basis. In rendering the opinion of the court on this matter, Chief Justice Warren said, among other things,

> Today, education is perhaps the most important function of the state and local governments. Compulsory school attendance laws and the great expenditures for education both demonstrate our recognition of the importance of education to our democratic society. . . . It is the very foundation of good citizenship. Today it is a primary instrument in awakening the child to cultural values, in preparing him for later professional training, and in helping him to adjust normally to his environment. . . . Such an opportunity, where the state has undertaken to provide it, is a right, which must be made available to all on equal terms.[13]

This court went further to state that separating the African-American students from their peers on the basis of race "generates a feeling of inferiority as to their status in the community that may affect their hearts and minds in a way unlikely ever to be undone."[14] It further stated that segregation of white and colored children in public education has a detrimental effect upon the colored children.[15] The court consequently ruled that the doctrine of Separate but Equal has no place in the U.S. educational system.

This landmark case broke the backbone of institutional segregation in the United States and opened the door for a fight for equality, which has continued till today. Sadly enough, some people think the fight is over. If the fight is over, we will not be discussing this issue any more. The next two cases are two significant indicators that the fight for equality has not really ended, and that the fight for equity is just beginning.

San Antonio Independent School District v. Rodriguez,
411 U.S. 1 (1973)

This landmark case was argued October 12, 1972. A group of Mexican-American parents brought a suit against this Texas school district in the summer of 1968 alleging that the school finance system of Texas, which was based on property tax, was unconstitutional as it violated the provisions of the Equal Protection Clause of the Fourteenth Amendment. The Edgewood Independent School District, from which these students came, was situated in the core-city section of San Antonio with little or no commercial property. The residents were predominantly Mexican-Americans (about 90 percent) with only 6 percent African-American students.

The average assessed value for homes in this community was $5,960, the lowest in the state. The district contributed $26 to the education of each child in the year 1967–1968, while the state foundation program contributed $222 per student, and the federal government contributed $108 per child, bringing the total amount of money spent on each child per year to $356.

When compared to Alamo Heights, the most affluent school district in San Antonio, with a population distribution of predominantly Anglos, 18 percent Mexican Americans, and less than 1 percent African Americans, spending $594 per pupil as a result of a strong property tax base, these plaintiffs argued that (1) the school financing in Texas discriminated against "poor" persons; (2) it discriminated against people who were relatively poorer than others; and (3) it discriminated against people who happened to reside in relatively poorer school districts, regardless of their personal income.[16]

In deciding this case, the lower court ruled that the Texas school finance system was unconstitutional, as it violated the provisions of the Fourteenth Amendment. The Supreme Court of the United States, however, ruled that the financing method employed (by the state of Texas) did not infringe upon any fundamental human right so as to call for the application of strict judicial scrutiny. In addition, the court did not view education as a fundamental right, which afforded explicit or implicit protection under the Constitution.

The initial ruling was consequently reversed and the state was cleared of the charges. It is significant to note the subtle but clear divergent views on the constitutional provisions for educational right as perceived by the judges in *Brown v. Board of Education* and in *San Antonio v. Rodriguez*. The issue at stake here is not as much a matter of equality as it is equity. Equity calls for giving each person what they need to succeed. Sadly, even the courts have difficulty defining what constitutes equal educational opportunities in the United States. Individual biases and prejudices play into every situation, and this has remained a major setback to equal educational opportunities in the United States.

Lau v. Nichols

The Supreme Court upheld that despite the fact that the Chinese students had the same caliber of teachers, textbooks, curriculum, and school facilities, they were being denied equal education because their unique language and cultural needs were not being met. In this case, the court discovered about 2,856 Chinese students in that public school system that did not speak the English language. Of this number, only 1,000 were given supplemental courses in English language. The rest—1,856—did not receive such support. The school district even required English-language skills before children could participate in educational programs. The Chinese parents of these students felt their children were receiving unequal educational opportunities. Part of the court ruling stated as follows:

> Discrimination among students on account of race or national origin that is prohibited includes "discrimination . . . in the availability or use of any academic . . . or other facilities of the grantee or other recipient." Discrimination is barred which has that effect even though no purposeful design is present. . . . It seems obvious that the Chinese-speaking minority receive fewer benefits than the English-speaking majority from respondents' school system which denies them a meaningful opportunity in the educational program.[17]

The Supreme Court reversed a previous appeal court ruling, agreeing with the plaintiffs that their children had not been provided equal educational opportunity as provided by the law, especially as provided under the Thirteenth Amendment.

To conclude our thoughts on these court landmarks, we will need to take a look at the Fourteenth Amendment to examine what it says about equal rights.

The Fourteenth Amendment

The Fourteenth Amendment to the Constitution of the United States of America has five different sections, each dealing with issues that relate to the rights of individual citizens in a participatory government, as well as the duties and obligations of the states and the nation to her naturalized or native-born citizens. The part of this amendment that has direct implications for the discussion in this section reads,

> All persons born or naturalized in the United States, and subject to the jurisdiction thereof, are citizens of the United States and of the State wherein they reside. No State shall make or enforce any law, which shall abridge the privileges or immunities of citizens of the United States; nor shall any State deprive any person of life, liberty, or property, without due process of law; nor deny to any person within its jurisdiction the equal protection of the laws.[18]

This amendment prevents any state from making or enforcing a law that abridges the privileges or immunities of citizens of the United States. It further prevents them from depriving any citizen of "life, liberty, or property" rights without due process of law. If the statement in the Supreme Court ruling on *Brown v. Board of Education of Topeka*, which says that educational opportunity "where the state has undertaken to provide it, is a right which must be made available to all on equal terms"[19] is taken to be true, it implies that in a nation where education is a mandate on the children, the right to a fair and equal education is no longer a privilege, but a constitutional right.

Once in a democratic government, the mandate is placed on the citizens to send their children to school until they reach a certain age, with the threat of punitive action, that government also places on itself the mandate of providing all children an equal and quality educational experience. Equal educational opportunities, therefore, can be simply defined as the provision of equitable educational facilities, personnel, resources, and learning experiences to every child, enabling that child to reach his or her maximum potential within the society.

The assumption of multicultural education is that the educational programs we have in place today fall short of this standard. American children do not enjoy equitable provision of educational facilities, personnel, resources, and learning experiences. About two decades ago, Jonathan Kozol went around many big American cities and studied the quality of education being provided to America's children. This research was published under the title *Savage Inequalities: Children in America's Schools* (1991).[20]

He opened our eyes to the sad reality that equality still does not exist in our educational systems, much less equity. The schools in affluent neighborhoods had the money to buy the resources necessary for student success. They had better and newer buildings, air-conditioning, science laboratories, gyms, and so forth, while their counterparts in the inner cities had to make do with structures that were hundreds of years old, with no heating, no air-conditioning, no science texts, no libraries—practically nothing. In many cases they were handed old and outdated textbooks that had been used by students in the richer neighborhoods, decades after the official end of Separate but Equal doctrine.

In Kozol's research, stories from all the cities sounded so much alike. The problems in New York were the same as in Chicago, San Antonio, New Jersey, and even Los Angeles. In East St. Louis, Missouri, students went to school on an active toxic dump. It all comes down to the "haves" and "have-nots." For the most part, the *haves* are the whites living in suburban America and the *have-nots* are the African Americans and Hispanics living in the inner cities. The race card comes up again!

When structured this way, the schools fail to fulfill their role as instruments for the propagation of knowledge and responsible citizenry. "It becomes striking how closely these schools reflect their communities, as if the duty of the schools were to prepare a child for life he's born to. . . . It hardly seems fair."[21] It also fails to foster upward mobility as promised by America.

Kozol's book was written in the 1990s, and one would expect that given all the publicity it received and the educational reforms we have seen in the past two decades, that things have changed dramatically. Sadly enough, a current look at the state of those schools still does not indicate equitable educational opportunities. Multicultural education calls for a time and context where America's children, whether rich or poor, African American or white, can learn in a clean classroom, use clean and current textbooks, and enjoy the privilege of learning under qualified teachers who care about their welfare and learning.

All our children need to grow up in an environment where they know that their only setback is their own personal dreams and aspirations, not the opportunities out there. This is not utopian thinking for a nation who enjoys a political, economic, and military strength that compares to none on the planet earth.

THE SPECTRUM OF INEQUITY IN EDUCATION

This section attempts to isolate the areas where we have continued to experience inequality in our educational system.

Curriculum Content

Over the years many battles have been fought over our curriculum content. The war has been waged from the gender angle, the racial/ethnic angle, and the ability/disability angle. For the most part, America's educational curriculum was essentially Eurocentric, male dominant, and insensitive to disabilities. Recently, state boards of education and school districts are beginning to respond to some of these challenges by requiring the writers of the textbooks to become more balanced. There still remains a problem. The need to be inclusive in the ethnic, gender, and ability makeup of our textbooks remains an area to which we can continue to make improvements.

Teacher Quality and Ethnic Makeup

Inner-city schools have always been laden with the burden of short-term inexperienced teachers who come there to start their careers only to transfer out as soon as they begin to get a handle on what they are doing. These schools have the endemic problem of inexperienced unqualified teachers teaching the sciences and mathematics. The quality of instruction going on in such schools is persistently subaverage, yet in this era of testing and accountability, these students are held to the same standards and expectations as the more successful suburban schools.

Even amid the requirements of the No Child Left Behind (NCLB) Act[22] and the current Every Student Succeeds Act (ESSA), inner-city schools are still struggling; to keep going, they must depend on a pool of inexperienced, under-qualified teachers.

Another issue is better articulated by Geneva Gay,[23] who said that "most graduates of typical teacher education programs know little about the cultural traits, behaviors, values, and attitudes that different children of color bring to the classroom, and how they affect students' responses to instructional situations."[24] Many inner-city schools are predominantly minority, while their teacher population has remained predominantly white, with little or no multicultural training. Unfortunately, a lot of these teachers still resist multicultural education. This questions their ability to meet the needs of students.

Buildings, Facilities, and Funds Allocation

The reforms of the last decade have led to many education bonds, which have resulted in facilities' restorations, construction, and modernization, yet many schools remain deprived of these face-lifts. Many poorer schools still lack heating and air-conditioning while their richer neighbors do not. Many states are taking a second look at how education is funded, and there is hope that more improvement is on the horizon, but we still have a long way to go.

Special Programs, Including GATE

Minority children, especially African-American boys, remain the highest population in special education programs, while the white students remain predominant in gifted and talented education (GATE) programs. Misinterpretation of cultural behaviors and perspectives remain a major issue in placements. According to James Banks (2004), "Many African American and Latino students who are labeled mentally retarded function normally and are considered normal in their homes and communities." Sadly, that's not the case when they get to school.

Assessments and Testing

Standardized testing has emerged as the only way the politicians can determine whether a school is doing well or not. Under the provisions of NCLB, schools that were not doing well risked getting shut down, while their more successful counterparts reaped financial rewards from the state. Even as Obama's Every Student Succeeds Act (ESSA) replaced NCLB, testing remains a major factor in evaluating school successes.

The sad reality is that every child does not come into the classroom with the same amount of educational capital, and given the sociocultural differences that we have referred to, it is simply unjust to hold them to the same standard when they are not all receiving equal education, much less equitable education.

FACTORS THAT INFRINGE ON EQUITY IN SCHOOLS

Social Class

More than race, social status has emerged as the leading variable in student achievement gap today. Children from affluent families have a tendency to do better than children from lower-income homes. Ironically, however, there is a racial dimension to it, as most people at the lower end of the socioeconomic structure are minorities and single mothers. Family status as a social issue, therefore, takes its own toll on the students, making equal educational opportunity more difficult as some students bring more to the classroom than others.

Parents' Education Level

Children from parents who have college education tend to do better at school than children whose parents are less educated. The support children get from home has a very definitive impact on how well they do in school. Many schools are operating on a scripted curriculum today and much of the instructional activities are one-directional: test-driven. Children whose parents are educated have the benefit of their parents discovering what is lacking in their education and working with them to bridge the gap. Parents with lower education would not know when their children are being deprived of meaningful learning experiences. How then would they be able to provide remediation outside of the classroom?

Racism

Racism remains a problem to contend with in today's schools. Institutional racism may be on the decline given the possibility of lawsuits and social isolation that accompanies such activities, but people's perspectives and mindsets don't change easily. Some individuals still go out of their way to give preferential treatment to particular students in academic situations. Tracking is one vehicle that racists have used to marginalize minority students over the years, and its residue remains in various forms in U.S. schools today.

School Culture

Every school has its own culture. Some school cultures encourage equity and social justice while others perpetuate inequality. Sometimes, inaction becomes an action. When school leadership fails to do something proactive to facilitate equity and social justice, it often becomes an unwritten approval for inequality. Schools must establish a climate that is empowering to all and make clear their disapproval of social inequity and injustice.

QUESTIONS AND APPLICATION

Case Study: Hispanics against Blacks

Background

You are the new principal of Jackson High School in South Central Los Angeles. Your school population is evenly split between African-American and Hispanic students, with a negligible number of whites and other minority groups. Jackson is known for her end-of-year gang warfare between African-American and Hispanic gangs. Last year the situation was so bad that the police had to come and shut down the school on the last day of school. This disrupted end-of-year programs that had been organized by many arms of the school. Many teachers and parents protested that action and consequently it led to the removal of the last principal. You have been brought in to straighten up things. You are known as a no-nonsense administrator. The district superintendent brought you here with a clear job description: the end of the gang rivalry at Jackson and improved academic achievement.

The Problem

You are African American. Upon arrival at Jackson, the Hispanic students and their parents immediately raised a protest. By replacing the white principal with an African American, it is seen as a victory for the African-American students and their parents. The Hispanic students and their parents vowed to make sure you are removed. They immediately began a petition drive and many openly expressed their disapproval of your appointment to you.

The Challenge

a. The district superintendent is aware of the resentment from the Hispanic community, but has decided he would not replace you, counting very much on your ability to turn things around. Would you want to convince him otherwise?

b. What action(s) would you take to gain the confidence of the Hispanic parents that you are not there as an advocate for the African-American students?
c. How would you work with the Hispanic students to gain their trust and confidence?
d. How can you build a bridge with the Hispanic community without at the same time burning the bridge that already exists with the African-American community due to common ethnicity? What would you do to ensure that the African American community does not see you as a "sell out"?
e. What would be your school-wide plan for reducing racial tensions? Present your first-, second-, and third-year plans.
f. What community activities would you undertake to further reduce ethnic tension among the parents?
g. Facilities, special programs, and testing are among the factors that continue to perpetuate inequality in schools. Discuss ways the local schools and the school districts can work around these challenges and still be able to meet the needs of their diverse student populations.

STRATEGIES FOR APPLICATION IN THE K–12 CLASSROOMS

1. *Grades K–12*: Work with your students to examine the main textbooks you use and determine the extent to which the various populations in your class are represented in the text being used. Brainstorm with your students on how to secure resources to balance the curriculum so that every group's contribution to that field is well represented.
2. *Grades K–12*: Lead your students to discuss the issue of discrimination. Have them create dioramas depicting their individual interpretations of discrimination. The diorama can be displayed at the school library for the school community to view.
3. *Grades 7–12*: Research and discuss migrant field workers and their issues, treatment, and abuse in the United States. Write reports, news briefs, and letters addressing your concerns for these workers and send to newspapers and legislators.

Chapter Six

Historical Foundations of Multicultural Education in the United States

---

Chapter Objectives:

This chapter explores the history of the development of multicultural education in the United States. It explores social and political developments, legal and legislative actions, educational developments, and the impacts of significant individuals toward this movement. Readers will be able to do the following:

1. Define multicultural education and trace its historical foundations
2. Discuss the impacts of the civil rights movement on the development of multicultural education
3. Discuss various legislations that impacted the development of the multicultural education movement in the United States
4. Identify the historical contributions of individuals such as John Ogbu, James Banks, and Jane Elliott toward the multicultural education movement

---

WHAT IS MULTICULTURAL EDUCATION?

Multicultural education has been defined in many ways along anthropological, sociological, philosophical, and psychological lines. Whereas the term may suggest a narrow focus on culture and cultural differences, the term "multicultural education" has been expanded over the years to include a vast array of diversity issues that span beyond culture to include gender, disability, and other diversity issues, thereby rendering the validity of the term itself questionable in its ability to encompass the vast array of issues that it addresses. Whereas most educators and sociologists have continued to use the term because of its historical significance, it is the opinion of this writer that the term "diversity" may be more embracing.

Nagai (2002) defined multicultural education as "an educational process or strategy involving more than one culture, as defined by national, linguistic, ethnic, or racial criteria."[1] It is seen as an attempt to create awareness and tolerance between cultures and related worldviews.

James Banks (2003) presents a more technical definition when he defined multicultural education as an idea, a process, and a reform movement.[2] According to him, multicultural education as an idea holds that all students—regardless of their gender, social class, ethnic, racial, or cultural characteristics—should have an equal opportunity to learn. The argument is that some students, because of race, gender, or social class, have a better chance to learn in schools as they are currently structured than do students who belong to other groups or who have different cultural characteristics.

Multicultural education as a process implies that it is not a one-shot activity. It is expected that it be an ongoing process that becomes an intrinsic part of the educational programs, not just a program or activity carried out at one point or the other. As a reform movement, it targets schools and educational systems with the intent of transforming them to the point that social class, gender, ethnicity, and languages do not pose a hindrance to any child from attaining his or her best potential in the schools. It calls for curricular changes as well as ideological changes.

The above definition of multicultural education is significant as we begin to explore its history and development. The question we are attempting to address here is this: "When and why did it became necessary to require the educational system to cater to the needs of all students represented in the school systems, and how has that attempt progressed over the years?"

HISTORICAL FOUNDATIONS OF MULTICULTURAL EDUCATION

The history of multicultural education in the United States does not enjoy the same deep roots that bilingual education can claim to the United States' early days. Whereas U.S. society has been multicultural from its earliest days, education and educational institutions have been essentially western in their structures and curricula. In its early days, U.S. society did not see education as a civil right; instead it was seen as a privilege reserved for a select few. Even among people from Western Europe, education (at least formal education) was not seen as a civil right; rather it was a privilege for those who could afford it. White women were denied equal access to formal education for many decades.[3]

Given that community schools were originally constituted along ethnic lines, the idea of multicultural education, which involved a heterogeneous student population and diverse curricula content, was out of the question. The only visible diversity that the educational system enjoyed from the early days was a diversity of Eurocentric curriculum, which included the study of German language, Latin, French, and other similar languages in English schools.

Exception, however, must be made for education pioneers like Horace Mann,[4] who in 1847 introduced the notion of universal public education as a worthy enterprise. Due to his influence and a number of other factors such as the need to stem the growing child labor that was endemic among immigrant populations, legislations for compulsory education came into effect in many states between 1852 and 1914.[5]

Reed Ueda (1993) makes reference to the existence of an "intercultural education"[6] program in the early 1920s.[7] He writes about a 1956 book by Jack Allen and Clarence Stegmeir, titled *Civics*, which reflected the trend toward endorsement of cultural pluralism in America. In this book they made the point that America is not a melting pot in which people of different origins mix and become one new and different people, but a place where good citizens live and work together in many groups. They advocated that the idea of a melting pot be discarded since America is a country where a variety of people have something of value to contribute.

Even though the U.S. Congress passed the Fourteenth and Fifteenth Amendments to the U.S. Constitution in 1870, guaranteeing civil rights and the right to vote to African Americans in the United States, the idea of education as a civil right did not actually become a popular opinion until the end of the Jim Crow[8] laws in the Southern states. Before the slave emancipation declaration, it was illegal to teach African Americans to read and write. Long after that law was rescinded, African Americans who got any education whatsoever got it from the hands of fellow African Americans and a few white abolitionists.

Whereas the years between 1865 and 1876 are regarded as the Reconstruction years—the period during which federal government laws provided civil rights protection for African Americans in the Southern states—the Jim Crow laws were in effect between 1876 and 1964. During this era, it was required by law in many states to provide separate educational and public facilities for whites and African Americans in the United States. In the state of Florida, for example, an 1895 education statute stated a penal offense for any person or school conducting public or private education where whites and colored people are taught in the same building or classroom. This statute had a penalty of between $150 and $500 or three to six months of imprisonment.

In the state of Mississippi, a similar law went as far as dictating that textbooks could not be used interchangeably between white and colored schools.

This was one of the worst states in the discriminatory practices.[9] Even with the *Brown v. Board of Education* ruling of 1954, which upheld the rights of every child (white or African American) to attend their neighborhood schools, laws were made by state and local school districts to circumvent this mandate, and up until 1964 many court cases were filed, tried, and ruled upon in response to *Brown*.

The movement toward multicultural education cannot claim a coordinated development that brought it about, yet many of the recent movements that have contributed to make it a reality can be traced back to the civil rights era. James Banks (2004)[10] articulates the dimensions and development of multicultural education in the United States under five subheadings: content integration, knowledge construction, equity pedagogy, prejudice reduction, and empowering school culture and social structure.

According to Banks (2004), the roots of content integration traces back to the works of an African-American scholar, George Washington Williams,[11] whose historical works date between 1882 and 1883. Banks traced knowledge construction to as far back as the 1960s in the works of revisionist social scientists, which were primarily people of color. Gary Nash (1993),[12] while not disputing the 1960s historical roots of the knowledge construction movements, indicates that in the 1990s the battle for cultural parity would be fought in the classrooms as African American and other minority parents sought to alter what their children were being taught in schools, a prediction that has proved to be true.

Banks (2004) traced prejudice reduction to 1920s researches on children's racial attitudes and traced equity pedagogy to the cultural deprivation paradigms of the 1960s.[13] Empowering school culture was traced to more recent works that focused on the needs of students from diverse ethnic, language, and racial groups and social classes.[14] Equity is identified as the basic rhetoric of the 1960s and provided the basis for both the integrationist movements and the movement toward gender equality in the United States.[15]

Regardless of the effects of the ideological elements identified by Banks, much of the 1970s and 1980s focused on desegregation and physical integration of African-American and white students in schools through busing, school choice, magnet schools, ratios, redrawing boundaries, intra- and interdistrict transfers, and many other similar activities.[16] Banks's *Handbook of Research on Multicultural Education* (2004) has a detailed discussion of these five dimensions and their significance to understanding multicultural education today.

The scope of this work would not allow a detailed engagement with those varied dimensions, but suffice it to say that whereas those dimensions focused on the ideological trends that provide foundational principles upon which we can build today, there were a number of other radical and more obvious developments that made multicultural education what it is in our time. Much of these are laws, movements, and initiatives that brought about radical revolutions that propelled us to where we are today in the push toward equality and equity pedagogy.

In the sections below we will investigate the various movements, laws, and individuals who have influenced the development of multicultural education both as "an idea, a process, and a reform movement" in the United States.

U.S. SOCIOPOLITICAL MOVEMENTS

The Civil Rights Movement—Legal Foundations

Most historians place the birth of the civil rights movement on May 17, 1954, when the U.S. Supreme Court ruled that a young African-American girl had the right to attend her neighborhood's white school. This ruling practically killed an 1896 court ruling, *Plessy v. Ferguson*,[17] which held that it was lawful to provide separate but equal educational facilities for whites and African Americans.

The significance of the *Brown v. Board of Education*[18] ruling lies in the fact that for the first time, the constitutional provisions of civil and voting rights given to African Americans under the law carried significance as the law now gives them equal access to educational facilities and resources.

As indicated earlier, this landmark ruling did not go unchallenged as many states and local school districts sought for ways to circumvent it. While this battle was still raging, Rosa Parks, an African-American woman, refused to give up her seat at the front of the bus to a white passenger on December 1 of the following year (1955).[19] She was arrested as was the law in Montgomery, Alabama, and this sparked an immediate reaction from the African-American community in the form of bus boycotts, which held its ground until December 21, 1956, when it ended with desegregation in buses.[20] This was the incident that propelled Dr. Martin Luther King Jr. to the limelight of the civil rights movement.

As the newly elected president of the Montgomery Improvement Association (MIA), King spearheaded the boycott. He soon joined with a number of other African-American leaders to found the Southern Christian Leadership Conference (SCLC) and was made its president. His organization became one of many such African-American movements advocating equal rights across the Southern states. Such movements as the Student Non-violent Coordinating Committee (SNCC), the Congress of Racial Equality (CORE), and the National Association for the Advancement of Colored People (NAACP) all played significant roles in the civil rights movement.[21]

Students' action in the civil rights movement may be of greater significance for the history of multicultural education. In September of 1957, nine African-American students showed up at all-white Central High School in Little Rock, Arkansas, and they were blocked from entering the school grounds by the order of the governor of the state. This attracted national attention, and the U.S. president, Dwight Eisenhower, had to send the National Guard to intervene on behalf of those students.

In Greensboro, North Carolina, four African-American students from the North Carolina Agricultural and Technical College launched a sit-in at a segregated restaurant, Woolworth's, but were refused service. This triggered similar sit-ins across the south. A large number of protesters and freedom riders of the civil rights movement were students.[22] On October 1, 1961, James Meredith, an African-American student, became the first person of African descent to enroll at the University of Mississippi. White segregationists reacted to his enrollment with violence and protests, compelling President Kennedy to send five thousand federal troops to restore calm.

The impact of these student-involved events, protests, acts of civil disobedience, and demand for fair treatment culminated in the 1964 Civil Rights Act, which was signed into law by President Lyndon Johnson on July 2, 1964, prohibiting discrimination on the basis of race, color, religion, or national origin. The impacts of the civil rights movement and the laws that followed it are more evident when you consider the fact that from the 1800s to 1968, African Americans were practically invisible in the major newspapers of major cities like Los Angeles (Barr 1993), but the movement propelled them to the front pages.

ETHNIC STUDIES MOVEMENTS

James Banks (2004) traces the roots of ethnic studies programs to the works of a number of African-American scholars[23] such as G. W. William (1882–1883), Woodson and Wesley (1922),[24] and W. E. B. Du Bois (1935, 1973).[25] Du Bois's work titled *Black Reconstruction in America* may be one of the major catalysts that have sensitized American historians to begin to look at American history from a more objective perspective, thus providing a strong basis for multicultural education.[26]

Ethnic studies programs as we know them today, however, can be regarded as a by-product of the civil rights movement. In the years following the Civil Rights Act (mostly the 1970s), educators began to advocate the inclusion of the history and interests of the other ethnic minorities in the school curriculum. Up until 1970, much of the U.S. educational curriculum had been essentially Eurocentric. Stories of most American peoples were omitted, and even the earliest Americans (Native Americans) were absent in the pages of many history books.

As minority students got more and more involved in the mainstream educational structures of the United States, they saw the need for the schools to speak to their own stories and struggles. The 1970s saw the birth of many ethnic studies programs across U.S. colleges and universities: African-American studies, Asian studies, and Hispanic studies programs. Even the story of Native Americans began to find its way into the mainstream educational curriculum.

Whereas these ethnic studies programs catered to the needs of the ethnic population in the colleges and universities, they were mostly sidelined, as often only ethnic minority people took these courses. So in effect, even though it brought in a divergent cultural view to the educational curriculum, it did not effectively infuse multiculturalism into the curriculum and into student life and culture. In many places these programs were isolated. The Reagan years from 1981 to the late 1980s were seen as an era in which ethnic studies programs suffered even further setbacks because the administration and its secretary of education, William Bennett, did not see much usefulness to these programs.[27]

Several other movements played roles in establishing the grounds on which multicultural education has now flourished. Such movements include the founding of various associations that have influenced educational policies and practices. Some of the organizations include the American Council on Education (ACE), the Anti-Defamation League (ADL), the National Education Association (NEA), and many others.[28] These organizations are known to have challenged the complex sociopolitical factors that have perpetuated inequality, prejudice, and discrimination.

COURT RULINGS AND GOVERNMENT LEGISLATIONS

Whereas laws do not change minds, laws and other government actions have remained the primary vehicles that have provided protection for minorities in the United States. It is sad to note that every one of the civil liberties enjoyed by minorities in the United States today came about after decades of struggles and battles in courts of law, Congress, or in the White House. This proves the assertion that those with power are never willing to share it. In this section, therefore, we will discuss landmark legal and congressional actions that have influenced the development of multicultural education in the United States.

Brown v. Board of Education of Topeka

This court case may be the most significant turning point in the fight for civil rights in U.S. history. The plaintiffs had argued as follows:

> Segregation of white and Negro children in the public schools of a state solely on the basis of race, pursuant to state laws permitting or requiring such segregation, denies the Negro children the equal protection of the laws guaranteed by the Fourteenth Amendment . . . even though physical facilities and other "tangible" factors of white and Negro schools may be equal. . . . Where a State has undertaken to provide an opportunity for an education in its public schools, such an opportunity is a right, which must be made available to all on equal terms. Segregation of children in public schools solely on the basis of race deprives children of the minority group equal educational opportunities, even though the physical facilities and other "tangible" factors may be equal.[29]

Thurgood Marshall, an African-American attorney, and a team of other highly qualified lawyers argued this case before the U.S. Supreme Court. In deciding this case, the U.S. Supreme Court ruled that in the field of public education, the doctrine of "Separate but Equal" has no rightful place as they are inherently unequal. The court further stated, "We have now announced that such segregation is a denial of the equal protection of the laws."

This ruling initiated sweeping educational and social reforms across the United States, and it can be arguably stated that on this day, multicultural education was born. For the first time, the U.S. courts placed their seal of approval on the Fourteenth Amendment of the Constitution, thereby laying a strong foundation for multicultural education.

The Civil Rights Act of 1964 (Title VII)

The general provisions of the Civil Rights Act of 1964 defines it as an act,

> [t]o enforce the constitutional right to vote, to confer jurisdiction upon the district courts of the United States to provide injunctive relief against discrimination in public accommodations, to authorize the attorney General to institute suits to protect constitutional rights in public facilities and public education, to extend the commission on Civil Rights, to prevent discrimination in federally assisted programs, to establish a Commission on Equal Employment Opportunity and for other purposes.[30]

The term programs include, but are not limited to, a college, university, other postsecondary institutions, secondary and elementary schools, or any other school system receiving any kind of federal funding. This act, and its sister, the 1965 civil rights bill, provided minorities a legal basis to demand equality with the white population. They outlawed discriminatory practices that had gone on for decades under the protection of the law, thereby setting the stage for minorities to demand equal treatment in educational settings as well as in the other public arenas for which the act and bill provided.

Equal Education Act of 1974

This act states that no state shall deny equal educational opportunity to any individual on the account of "race, color, sex, or national origin." This act provided a broad protection from many discriminatory practices including the following:

- the deliberate segregation by an educational agency of students on the basis of race, color, or national origin among or within schools;
- the failure of an educational agency which has formerly practiced such deliberate segregation to take affirmative steps, consistent with part 4 of this subchapter, to remove the vestiges of a dual school system;
- the assignment by an educational agency of a student to a school, other than the one closest to his or her place of residence within the school district in which he or she resides, if the assignment results in a greater degree of segregation of students on the basis of race, color, sex, or national origin among the schools of such agency than would result if such student were assigned to the school closest to his or her place of residence within the school district of such agency providing the appropriate grade level and type of education for such students; [and]
- the failure by an educational agency to take appropriate action to overcome language barriers that impede equal participation by its students in its instructional programs.[31]

This act was preceded by the 1972 Title IX Education Amendment, which, among other things, outlawed discrimination on educational opportunities on the basis of gender. Women in the U.S. gained legal rights to attend schools of their choices and pursue educational programs of choice without discrimination.

Such lawsuits as *Lau v. Nichols* (1974) in California, and *San Antonio Independent School District v. Rodriguez* (1973) projected the damaging effects of discriminatory practices and legal prohibitions that lead to inequity in educational opportunities as well as the resistance struggles that accompanied them. The proximity of these two landmark cases to this law makes clear its timeliness to reduce tension that was already mounting in many parts of the nation. Equal educational opportunity became a legal right, and for some years the debate centered on a definition of equal educational opportunities, a debate that is still ongoing.

SCHOLARS AND EDUCATORS—
INTELLECTUAL FOUNDATIONS

Laws do not change minds, neither do they reduce prejudices, but they are necessary parameters that censor actions in a civilized society. Whereas the laws have made the general provisions for the pursuit of equality and multicultural education, multiple scholars and academicians have produced research insights that are changing minds, attitudes, and behaviors, making the provisions of law more acceptable to people in such a pluralistic democracy as the United States of America. In the time period following the 1970s, scholars and academicians have championed the journey toward implementation of equal educational opportunities and multicultural education.

A cursory glance reveals certain names whose contributions have been significant. James Banks (2004) identified a number of these people, himself included, with others such as L. D. Delpit, J. Ogbu, B. J. Shade, Michael Harrington, Jane Elliott, and many others.

From outside of the United States, Paulo Freire published his *Pedagogy of the Oppressed* in 1970, and *Education for Critical Consciousness* in 1973.[32] These two works had a radical impact on education and the social climate of schools. It became obvious that educational structures that do not have liberating effects fall short of the ideal. Other Latin-American liberation movements—some of which found expression in liberation theology, black liberation, and black theology in the United States and South Africa—and other similar influences may have had their own impacts.

By the late 1970s, it was becoming clear that the purpose of education was not only to provide learning and skills development but empowerment, which allowed the recipients of educational programs to critique their environment, question issues, and actively engage in social and civic life.

We will outline a brief summary of the contributions of some of these individuals as we conclude this chapter.

James Banks

James Banks is the Kerry and Linda Killinger Professor of Diversity Studies and director of the Center for Multicultural Education at the University of Washington in Seattle. His areas of specialization are multicultural education and social studies education. One of his significant contributions to the field of multicultural education is his "Approaches to Curriculum Reform," which outlines four levels of multicultural education: the Contributions approach, the Additive approach, the Transformation approach, and the Social Action approach. He articulated levels three and four as the most effective ways to implement multicultural education curriculum.[33]

Banks is probably the most published scholar in the United States in the field of multicultural education. A list of some of his significant works are referenced in the bibliography of this book.

1969 —"A Content Analysis of the African American in Textbooks." *Social Education* 33, 954–57, 963.
1970 —*Teaching the African American Experience: Methods and Materials* (Belmont, CA: Fearon).
1973 —*Teaching Ethnic Studies: Concepts and Strategies* (43rd yearbook). J. A. Banks (ed.). Washington, DC: National Council for Social Studies.
1984 —"African American Youths in Predominantly White Suburbs: An Exploratory Study of Their Attitudes and Self-Concepts." *Journal of Negro Education* 53, 3–17.
1988 —"Ethnicity, Class, Cognitive, and Motivational Styles: Research and Teaching Implications." *Journal of Negro Education* 57, 452–66.
1991 —"The Dimensions of Multicultural Education." *Multicultural Leader* 4, 5–6.
1991 —"Multicultural Education: Its Effects on Students' Ethnic and Gender Role Attitudes." In J. P. Shaver (ed.), *Handbook of Research on Social Studies Teaching and Learning* (New York: Macmillan), 459–69.
1992 —"Multicultural Education: Approaches, Developments, and Dimensions." In J. Lynch, C. Modgil, and S. Modgil (eds.), *Cultural Diversity and the Schools, Vol. 1, Education for Cultural Diversity: Convergence and Divergence* (London: Falmer Press), 83–94.
1993 —"The Canon Debate, Knowledge Construction, and Multicultural Education." *Educational Researcher* 22, no. 5, 4–14.
1993 —"Multicultural Education for Young Children: Racial and Ethnic Attitudes and Their Modification." In B. Spodek (ed.), *Handbook of Research on the Education of Young Children* (New York: Macmillan), 236–50.
1996 —*Multicultural Education: Transformative Knowledge, and Action: Historical and Contemporary Perspectives* (New York: Teachers College Press).
1998 —"The Lives and Values of Researchers: Implications for Educating Citizens in a Multicultural Society." *Educational Researcher* 27, no. 7, 4–17.
2001 —*Cultural Diversity and Education: Foundations, Curriculum and Teaching*. 4th ed. (Boston: Allyn & Bacon).
2003 —"Approaches to Multicultural Curricular Reform." In J. A. Banks and C. A. M. Banks (eds.), *Multicultural Education: Issues and Perspectives*. 4th ed., rev. (New York: John Wiley & Sons), 225–46.
2003 —"Multicultural Education: Characteristics and Goals." In J. A. Banks and C. A. M. Banks (eds.), *Multicultural Education: Issues and Perspectives*. 4th ed., rev. (New York: John Wiley & Sons), 3–30.
2003 —*Teaching Strategies for Ethnic Studies*. 7th ed. (Boston: Allyn & Bacon).
2003 —*Multicultural Education: Issues and Perspectives*. 4th ed., rev. Edited by J. A. Banks and C. A. M. Banks (New York: John Wiley & Sons).
2004 —*Handbook of Research on Multicultural Education*. 2nd ed. Edited by J. A. Banks and C. A. M. Banks (San Francisco: John Wiley & Sons).

John Ogbu

John Ogbu, a Nigerian-born scholar who passed away in 2003, is described in an obituary statement as "a professor of anthropology at the University of California, Berkeley, and a path-breaking scholar in the fields of minority education and identity."[34] He attempted to understand and explain how racial and ethnic diversity influenced achievement educationally and economically. He focused primarily on differential educational achievement of minority students in the United States.

As an anthropologist, Ogbu undertook a series of primary research that targeted minority groups. A long list of scholarly works is attributed to Ogbu, including the following:[35]

2003 —*African American Students in an Affluent Suburb: A Study of Academic Disengagement* (Mahwah, NJ: Lawrence Erlbaum).

2002 —"African-American Students and the Academic Achievement Gap: What Else You Need to Know." *Journal of Thought* 37, no. 4, 9–33.

2001 —"Cultural Amplifiers of Intelligence" (with P. Stern). In *Understanding Race and Intelligence*. Edited by J. Fish (Mahwah, NJ: Lawrence Erlbaum).

2001 —"Caste Status and Intellectual Development" (with P. Stern). In *Environmental Effects on Cognitive Abilities*. Edited by R. J. Sternberg and E. Grigorenko (Mahwah, NJ: Lawrence Erlbaum), 1–37.

2000 —"Collective Identity and Schooling" (in Japanese). In *Education, Knowledge and Power*. Edited by H. Fujita (Tokyo, Japan: Shinyosha Ltd.).

1999 —"Beyond Language: Ebonics, Proper English, and Identity in a African-American Speech Community." *American Educational Research Journal* 36, no. 2 (Summer).

1999 —"Cultural Context of Children's Development." *In Children of Color: Research, Health, and Policy Issues*. Edited by H. E. Fitzgerald, B. M. Lister, and B. S. Zuckerman (New York: Garland), 73–92.

1998 —"Voluntary and Involuntary Minorities: A Cultural-Ecological Theory of School Performance with Some Implications for Education" (with H. D. Simons). *Anthropology and Education Quarterly* 29, no. 2, 155–88.

1997 —"Speech Community, Language Identity and Language Boundaries." In *Language and Environment: A Cultural Approach to Education for Minority and Migrant Students*. Edited by A. Sjogren (Stockholm, Sweden: Botkyrka. B), 17–42.

1997 —"Racial Stratification in the United States: Why Inequality Persists." In *Education: Culture, Economy, and Society*. Edited by A. H. Halsey, H. Lauder, P. Brown, and A. S. Wells (Oxford: Oxford University Press).

1997 —"Understanding the School Performance of Urban African Americans: Some Essential Background Knowledge." In *Children and Youth: Interdisciplinary Perspectives*. Edited by H. J. Walberg, O. Reyes, and R. P. Weissberg.

1997 —Foreword to "Reconstructing 'Dropout': A Critical Ethnography of the Dynamics of African American Students' Disengagement from School," by G. J. S. Dei, J. Mazzuca, E. McIsaac, and J. Zine (Toronto: University of Toronto Press).
1996 —"Educational Anthropology." In *Encyclopedia of Cultural Anthropology.* Vol. 2. (New York: Henry Holt and Company), 371–77.
1994 —"Culture and Intelligence." In *Encyclopedia of Intelligence.* Edited by R. Stenberg (New York: MacMillan), 328–38.
1993 —"Differences in Cultural Frame of Reference." *International Journal of Behavioral Development* 16, no. 3, 483–506.

Paulo Freire

Freire was a Brazilian educator who spent his life working with the poor and marginalized in Latin America. Freire operated from a conviction that the poor in Latin America had been denied basic human rights, and his work projected the rift that had existed between the historical social classes of Latin America into the center of academic dialogue (Conti 1977).[36]

Freire wrote that Latin American societies were established as "closed societies" (1998, 505)[37] right from the time of European conquests. He argued that the common people were held in bondage by a high percentage of illiteracy, diseases, alarming rates of infant mortality, malnutrition, and high crime rates, factors he easily associated with underdevelopment and dependency.

Freire described the societies as characterized by rigid hierarchical social structures that lacked internal markets, anchored on a "precarious and selective educational system" whose schools served as instruments to maintain the status quo (p. 505).[38] He believed that the oppression of the poor had led to the poor being alienated from personal decision-making processes, and to their accepting and settling with their personal inferiority and inability to make personal decisions.

Freire operated from a conviction that the poor could achieve their own humanization by becoming more aware of their selfhood and by acting to transform their society. He pointed out that by erroneously believing that their security lay in the system that oppressed them, the poor and marginalized feared freedom and the risk of change (Conti 1977).[39]

So Freire proposed that education need no longer continue to be an instrument of oppression and dehumanization; rather it should become a vehicle by which students are able to come to a critical understanding of their situation and engage in efforts to transform their situations and their societies. He came up with the idea of "conscientization," in which students are able to begin to question the world around them, begin to engage in dialogue so as to decode the reality around them in a systematic way, and to stop their own oppression and transform the conditions around them toward their own liberation (Sleeter, Torres, and Laughlin 2004).[40]

Freire stressed on dialogue in education as a way to effect understanding and to change and facilitate both literacy and social transformation (Wade 1998).[41] Freire saw the vital role of the progressive educator as unveiling the opportunities for hope for the marginalized, regardless of the power of the forces that tend to keep them marginalized (Friedland 2004).[42] Among the many works of Freire are the following:

1998 —*Pedagogy of Freedom: Ethics, Democracy, and Civic Courage* (Lanham, MD: Rowman & Littlefield).
1998 —*Politics and Education* (Los Angeles: UCLA Latin American Center).
1998 —*Teachers as Cultural Workers: Letters to Those Who Dare Teach* (Boulder, CO: Westview).
1997 —*Mentoring the Mentor: A Critical Dialogue with Paulo Freire* (New York: P. Lang).
1997 —*Pedagogy of the Heart* (with A. M. A. Freire; New York: Continuum).
1994 —*Pedagogy of Hope: Reliving Pedagogy of the Oppressed* (with A. M. A. Freire; New York: Continuum).
1993 —*Pedagogy of the City* (New York: Continuum).
1993 —*Pedagogy of the Oppressed* (New York: Continuum).
1988 —*Teachers as Intellectuals: Towards a Critical Pedagogy of Learning* (with H. Giroux and P. McLaren; Granby, MA: Bergin and Garvey).
1987 —*Freire for the Classroom: A Sourcebook for Liberators Teaching* (with I. Shore; Portsmouth, NH: Boynton/Cook.)
1987 —*Cultural Wars: School and Society in the Conservative Restoration 1969–1984* (with I. Shore; London: Routledge & Kegan Paul).
1987 —*Literacy: Reading the Word and the World* (with D. P. Macedo; South Hadley, MA: Bergin and Garvey).
1985 —*The Politics of Education: Culture, Power, and Liberation* (South Hadley, MA: Bergin and Garvey).
1978 —*Pedagogy in Process: The Letters to Guinea-Bissau* (New York: Continuum/Seabury Press).
1976 —*Education, the Practice of Freedom* (London: Writers and Readers Publishing Cooperative).
1975 —*Conscientization* (Geneva: World Council of Churches).
1973 —*Education for Critical Consciousness* (New York: Seabury).
1970 —*Cultural Action for Freedom* (Cambridge: Harvard Educational Review).
1970 —*Pedagogy of the Oppressed* (New York: Continuum).

Jane Elliott

A mother of four children and a third-grade teacher at the Riceville, Iowa, community elementary school, Elliott was not a household name until 1968 when she began to take a radical step to address the issues of racial discrimination and inequality within the four walls of her own classroom.

It was on the day following the death of Dr. Martin Luther King Jr. that she began to carry out an exercise that was soon to revolutionize her classroom, raise protests from some whites in her community, and bring lots of insults, abuse, attacks, and ostracism her way. This activity, which she called "Blue Eye, Brown Eye," addressed racial discrimination based on skin color, eye color, and hair texture and color.

The activity turned the table of discrimination on the light-skinned blue-eyed kids in her classroom, and she gave them a one-day's taste of what it feels like to be discriminated against. Both the controversies and rejections she attracted as a result of this activity propelled her to public view when in 1970 her classroom activity of "Blue Eyes, Brown Eyes" was featured on ABC News under the title "Eye of the Storm."

Since that time Elliott has spent her time teaching and lecturing on the impact of racial discrimination, and her videos and lecture materials are used across the nation in many classrooms. She has taken her lectures and activities beyond the shores of the United States of America and has continued to change people's perspectives as she confronts people with the harmful reality of discrimination.[43]

Elliott's works have been produced in videos to spread her one-person campaign for racial tolerance. Some of the videos include the following: *Eye of the Storm* (ABC News) 1970, *A Class Divided* (1984), *Blue Eyed* (1996), *Essential Blue Eyed* (1996, revised 1999), *The 30 Minute Blue Eyed* (1996), *The Angry Eye* (2001), *Indecently Exposed* (2005), and *The Stolen Eye* (2002).

Elliott's radical approach to multicultural education has penetrated unusual places in the United States, such as police academies, public-service arenas, and institutions of higher learning.

QUESTIONS AND APPLICATION

Case Study: Teaching at Abbot High

Background

You are the new history teacher at Abbot High School. Abbot High is one of the most reputable high schools in the nation. Known for its high academic standards and a history of highly successful alumni, you are expected to carry on a one-hundred-year-old tradition of high academic excellence and uncompromising commitment to a high level of integrity.

Most teachers at Abbot have been there for twenty years or more. People rarely leave Abbot to go to another school, as it would be seen as a demotion. They are meticulous in their selection of teachers, and they always hire the cream of the crop. Coming into Abbot at your youthful age, people see you as highly privileged and specially favored. The older teachers continuously remind you of how lucky you are to join them and how happy they are to have you.

Parents tell you that you are privileged to be hired at Abbot, and that they know you will prove worthy of the honor. The school, while mostly white with a very insignificant number of blacks and Asians and not a single Hispanic, espouses to be color blind in their policy toward racial and cultural integration. People are supposed to be seen as people and not as racial groups or cultural groups.

The Problem

During your first week at Abbot, you take the time to go through the adopted textbooks that you are required to teach from. You are shocked to realize that most of the texts, while new, follow an old tradition of male-dominated curriculum; females and minority figures are conspicuously absent in the pages of the history books.

The curriculum is a very dominant, white male curriculum. The culture of the school is a dominant Anglo-Saxon male culture. The minority students are often called names, but they cannot protest for fear of raising issues and being kicked out of this highly respected high school. You have been thoroughly immersed in multicultural education, and you strongly believe that the curriculum should be balanced ethnically and genderwise.

The Challenge

a. What modifications would you make in your text selection, curriculum content, and instructional strategies?
b. Would you confront the school authorities with your impression of the adopted texts? Why? Why not?
c. Should you choose to confront them with the problems with the adopted texts, how would you describe the problems to them? What would be your rationale for requiring a review of the adopted texts? What compromises are you willing to make concerning the texts and your convictions and beliefs in a balanced curriculum?
d. Should you fail to convince them to change the adopted texts, what would you do to make up for the lack of balance in the curriculum? What risks do you run when you include materials that are not part of the adopted texts?
e. Would you choose to engage the school with the racial insensitivity that you are observing? If you choose to address it, how would you start? What risks do you run as you choose to engage this topic?
f. What convincing arguments can you put across to the school authorities on the major weakness of the color-blind approach to cultural integration?

REVIEW QUESTIONS

a. What would you consider the foundational developments that gave birth to multicultural education in the United States?
b. In what unique ways was the civil rights movement a catalyst toward the development of multicultural education?
c. In what ways did sociopolitical movements help to advance multicultural education?
d. Who would you consider the intellectual forerunners of the multicultural education movement? What were their unique contributions to this movement?
e. Which landmark legislations had the most profound impact on the advancement of multicultural education in the United States? How did they advance multicultural education?

STRATEGIES FOR APPLICATION

1. *Grades K–6*: Read the stories of Linda Brown and Harriett Tubman and discuss with the class how these individuals helped to change our society into a better place. Discuss problems of discrimination and oppression that still exist in our society today and even at the school and let students brainstorm ways they can make a difference.
2. *Grades 7–12*: Provide students with or ask them to go on the internet and research different versions of Jim Crow laws. Create opportunities for students to read, analyze, and discuss these laws in the context of civil rights. Allow them to identify and discuss factors that would lead to such laws in any given society and what is wrong about those laws.
3. *Grades 7–12*: Allow students to research the history and controversies surrounding affirmative action. Structure an informed debate on the pros and cons of affirmative action for the twenty-first century. Allow students to come up with what could be a reasonable alternative to affirmative action in the twenty-first century.

Chapter Seven

Standards-Based Planning and Teaching in a Multicultural Classroom

---

Chapter Objectives:

This chapter provides foundational principles for standards-based planning and teaching in a multicultural classroom. It provides a step-by-step approach to planning and teaching a multicultural lesson. It also showcases a model multicultural lesson and other resources needed by K–12 teachers. Readers will be able to do the following:

1. Become familiar with standards-based planning and teaching
2. Describe Banks's four levels of multicultural education
3. Identify the basic factors and elements that make for differentiated instruction
4. Explain the seven-step lesson plan and vital elements needed in each section in planning a multicultural lessons.
5. Define a social action objective, and be able to articulate a social action objective for a given lesson
6. Create a social action project as a culminating activity for a multicultural lesson plan

---

STANDARDS-BASED PLANNING AND TEACHING

The conversation around standards-based planning and teaching can be said to have reached its plateau in the American educational discourse. With the adoption of the Common Core State Standards in about forty-two U.S. states, along with the District of Columbia, this conversation is no longer sectional.

Reaching a critical mass in the 1990s, the discussion on standardization of the educational curriculum in the K–12 educational settings was mostly responsible for the landmark educational reform of the George W. Bush administration, the "No Child Left Behind" act of 2001. The enactment of this act changed the educational culture and landscape in America.

As the United States was entering the twenty-first century, the conversation on the future of education focused on the ability, or lack thereof, of American students to compete healthily with their peers in other developed countries. This concern was coupled with the discussion on the skills and competencies students would need for success in the workplace as well as their readiness for college.

By the year 2002, a movement was born, known as the Partnership for 21st Century Learning. This was a coalition of the business community, nonprofits, educational leaders, and policymakers, who came together around a national conversation on the importance of twenty-first-century skills for all students. This group developed a framework for twenty-first-century learning, which is represented in figure 7.1.

Skills such as creativity, innovation, critical thinking, problem solving, communication, and collaboration were identified as critical skills twenty-first-century learners must possess to be ready for college and work. In 2007, the National Governors Association (NGA) and the Council of Chief State School Officers (CCSSO) released a report indicating that to achieve a world-class education for American students, there needed to be a common benchmark for all students.

Two years later in 2009, governors and state commissioners of education in forty-eight U.S. states launched a movement toward a common national

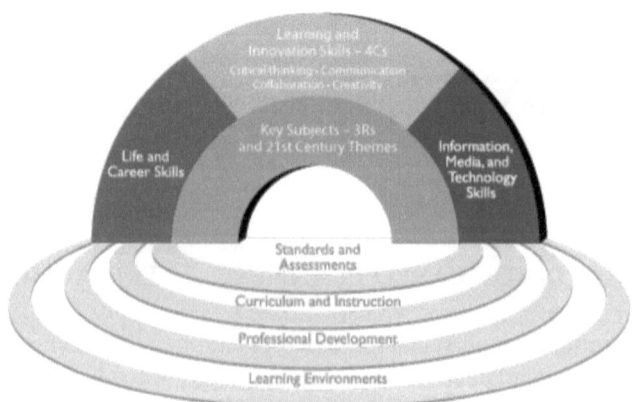

Figure 7.1. Framework for Twenty-First-Century Learning

standard. This is the movement that led to the creation of the Common Core State Standards (CCSS). The goal was to develop a uniform and consistent set of standards that would ensure that U.S. students, upon completion of their high school education, were properly equipped with the skills and competencies they would need for college and career.

In the process of developing these standards, this body relied heavily on teachers and standards experts from across the country. This common standard was released in June of 2010, and by August of 2015, forty-two U.S. states had adopted the standards (Common Core State Standards Initiative 2016). While the debates and conversations on the quality and effectiveness of the Common Core State Standards continues in the political and academic arenas, the question of the relevance of uniform standards for the American educational setting seems to be giving way to these other arguments. It appears that standards-based planning and teaching are here to stay in the American educational environment.

MULTICULTURAL EDUCATION AND STANDARDS-BASED PLANNING AND TEACHING

Tension has developed between the standards movement in the United States and multicultural education. This tension is only one of the oppositions facing the future of education today. According to Thompson (2001), "[o]ne thing the standards movement will never be accused of is a lack of critical opposition."[1] Some educators and critics tend to see an irreconcilable polarity between the standards movement and the multicultural education movement. A question that must be addressed, however, is whether such a polarity exists.

Thompson (2001) argues that there is a mistaken assumption that authentic standards-based reform, and test-based reforms are one and the same thing. He defined authentic standards-based reform as "fundamentally concerned with equity," and radically departs from tracking and what he calls the "factory-style school,"[2] which is evident in test-based reforms. Standards-based instruction, distinct from test-based reform can be defined for the purposes of this work as instructional practices that anchor on a state-approved guide, which outlines essential learning and curriculum content for every grade level from kindergarten to twelfth grade.

Resistance that has been rightly directed toward the standards movement is a reaction against the accompanying standardized tests. The reasons for such resistance are many, including (1) the fact that standardized tests are inaccurate measures of learning; and (2) standardized testing hijacks instruction and converts it to test preparation, instead of real learning for students.[3]

It is difficult to argue against the standardization of learning and curriculum alone—a necessary evil that has become part of the school system as we experience more and more governmental involvement. Some, however, have successfully argued against it on political grounds because they feel that standardization takes away local control of school curriculum. In 2016, Donald Trump won the presidency on the basis of many conservative agendas, which included doing away with the Common Core State Standards. The possibility of pursuing standards at the expense of real individual needs of students is what makes it a little more difficult for many educators to subscribe fully to the standards movement.

One of the fundamental points of confusion in understanding standards-based instruction is the assumption that it suggests a one-size-fits-all approach to teaching. A series of studies cited by Wang and Odell (2002) provide a variety of ways for looking at standards-based teaching. They cited Romberg (1992), Cobb (1994), and Cohen (1984) as presenting standards-based instruction as student-centered instruction that focuses on progressive ideas and constructivist ideas of learning and constructing knowledge, as active sense-making by students, and as collaborative inquiry.

According to them, knowledge is seen as "consisting of cultural artifacts constructed by individuals and groups."[4] If these ideas of standards-based instruction are to be taken seriously, one can logically argue that there might be a positive relationship that exists between standards-based instruction and multicultural education, contrary to the general perception.

According to Beverly Falk (2002), standards-based instruction and assessments can sometimes stimulate teachers and their students to "get clear about their purposes, to develop coherent goals for learning, and to make use of a range of instructional strategies to support students' varying approaches to learning."[5] A more appropriate argument is that high standards, when required for all, may make it possible to invest resources into helping those who need extra help.[6]

The argument must be presented, however, that despite the possible symbiotic relationship that may be found between the standards-based instructional reform and the multicultural education movement, multicultural education seems to have suffered grave casualties in states where the standards-based reform movement has been the strongest.

One of the fundamental issues that has often crippled the implementation of multicultural education in today's classrooms is that there is no time for another "subject." Many teachers and school administrators mistakenly look at the idea of multicultural education as the inroad of a new subject into the school curriculum. This misperception of multicultural education is based on the forms multicultural education has traditionally taken in schools.

James Banks (2003) presented four levels of multicultural education in his work—Contributions, Additive, Transformation, and Social Action approaches. According to him, the first level, Contributions, deals with heroes, holidays, and discrete cultural elements. Teachers conveniently infuse cultural issues like holidays and heroes into their curriculum.

Banks refers to this approach as the easiest approach for teachers to integrate multicultural content into their curriculum, but one may argue against that assumption, because amid the contemporary, standards-based instructions, "scripted teaching," "pacing," and "bench-marking," it is more and more difficult to integrate cultural contributions and holidays into the main curriculum, unless it comes with the scripted teaching package.

At the second level, the Additive approach, teachers add content, concepts, themes, and perspectives that are multicultural without changing the structure of their instructional materials. Teachers work hard to infuse multicultural themes, contents, and perspectives into the main curriculum. When many teachers do this, it often involves worksheets and reading materials on specific cultural activities related to the main topic being taught. The problem with this approach is that whereas it may work perfectly well in history and social studies or language arts classes, it may be hard to do in mathematics, science, and other technical classes.

In mathematics and science classrooms, you may see multicultural games used to teach mathematics or science concepts (e.g., Mankala [Okwe], an African game used in teaching addition, subtraction, and multiplication). When such games are used, their multicultural emphases are often lost as nothing is done or said to connect the activity to the culture from which it originated.

The contemporary standards-based curriculum is crammed with lots of reading, writing, and arithmetic, as schools are struggling to meet the various state academic standards as well as score high on high-stakes tests. It is known that local schools should hold the power on how they constitute and deliver instruction.[7]

With the standards movement and its accompanying evils of pacing and scripted teaching, that right and power has been significantly taken away from schools; requiring them to spend extra time teaching heroes and holidays, as well as multicultural games, is to require the impossible from them. Besides the lack of time and space in the curriculum, the first two approaches have little or no value in transforming students' worldview or enhancing cultural appreciation, respect, and tolerance. The first two approaches are superficial, and they place additional demands on teaching time and curriculum space.

In this age of standards-based instruction and assessments, any attempt to implement multicultural education, which follows the first level, will require a significant curriculum adjustment as teachers would be required to teach heroes, holidays, and cultural events outside of the main adopted state academic content standards. Some types of academic activities that take place as a part of the cultural emphasis program are done as extracurricular activities rather than as part of the academic curriculum. When it is done as part of the academic curriculum, it might be through the use of worksheets that have little or no connection to the academic standards.

It is indeed an additional piece of work, which many teachers don't have time and resources to undertake, given the pressures they face now. The second level is an improvement over the first, but remains significantly insufficient for today's classroom, as many schools are demanding that all learning activities be tied to the academic content standards. When teachers realize that even though the multicultural activity would be relevant and helpful to students, if it is not clearly tied to the standards, they would be reluctant to have their supervisors walk in on them doing an activity that they cannot readily link to the standards.

The last two approaches—the Transformation approach and the Social Action approach, do not necessarily require a separate curriculum. According to Banks (2003), in these two approaches, "ethnic content is added to the mainstream core curriculum without changing its basic assumptions, nature, and structure."[8] It is also at these two levels that we can see the possibility of integrating standards-based instruction and multicultural education.

First, let's look at the two levels. The Transformation approach requires teachers to change the structure of their curriculum to enable students to engage concepts, issues, events, and themes from a multicultural perspective. Here teachers use the mainstream subject areas like mathematics, the arts, language, and literature to acquaint students with the ways the common U.S. culture and society has "emerged from a complex synthesis and interaction of the diverse cultural elements that originated within the various cultural, racial, ethnic, and religious groups that make up U.S. society."[9] Here students engage and critique issues and concepts that deal with diversity and social justice. They learn to take a stand.

Banks's fourth level of multicultural education, the Social Action approach, "allows students to make decisions on important social issues and take actions to help solve them."[10] The last two approaches are best implemented by weaving culture appreciation and cultural awareness issues into the existing curriculum: Mathematics, language arts, history/social studies, and science. Using this approach, the teachers are able to teach the standards and follow whatever pacing guides are stipulated by their districts while teaching equity and social justice without having to look for extra time in their day to teach multicultural awareness.

It is in the planning of their instruction for the basic subjects that teachers are able to weave in multicultural education. A legitimate question that follows would be "how can we do this?" The fact that this can be done, and the fact that instruction can be delivered at the highest level of cultural integration, makes it a better approach; it could prove to be the most effective and yet least time-consuming approach to teaching both standards and multicultural education. It does not require separate or additional time for planning and teaching.

DIFFERENTIATED INSTRUCTION

Differentiation is a foundational instructional approach that must underscore teacher activity in any multicultural classroom. Some educators have defined differentiated instruction as "a process where educators vary the learning activities, content demands, and modes of assessment to meet the needs and support the growth of each child."[11]

To fully understand the unique elements of differentiated instruction, we must pay particular attention to the phrase "each child." The attempt to differentiate instruction is done with due recognition and respect for the variance that exists among individual learners in any given classroom.[12]

According to Tomlinson (2000), differentiated instruction occurs when teachers become increasingly proficient in understanding their students as individuals, as they become increasingly comfortable with the meaning and structure of the disciplines they teach, and as they increasingly become experts at teaching flexibility in order to match instruction to student needs with the goal of maximizing the potential of each learner in a given area.[13] To reach this level of expertise, beginning-level teachers must purposefully engage the task of differentiating instruction.

In a position paper by Liliana Salazar et al. (2004), two primary obstacles that prevent teachers from individualizing their instructional practices were identified as lack of space and lack of training. Discussing lack of space, they stated that in schools where overcrowding exists, teachers do not have enough classroom space to warrant individualized instruction because in some such schools two teachers end up sharing one classroom space. Trainings available to educators on differentiated instruction (DI) have been limited and inadequate in many instances.

Many veteran teachers who are not used to DI may not have lots of opportunities and resources to avail themselves of the training. Additionally, many newly trained teachers are unable to do it because they have not been adequately prepared for it in the teacher preparation programs.

There are four areas where teachers can differentiate instruction: content, process, products, and learning environment (Tomlinson 2000). A significant element of differentiated instruction is that it enables teachers to challenge all learners at their individual ability levels. Instruction is planned and delivered within individual students' zone of proximal development.

Tomlinson (1999)[14] suggests that differentiated instruction is not an instructional strategy or a teaching style, but is a way of thinking about teaching and learning. This way of thinking about teaching begins with the student population in mind, not the subject matter or the content area. Tomlinson identified four main characteristics of a differentiated classroom as (1) a context for focused and principle-driven instruction, (2) ongoing assessment, (3) consistent flexibility, and (4) a context that allows students to become active explorers with the teacher as a guide (Tomlinson 1995).[15]

Differentiated instruction (DI) flourishes in educational environments that use performance-based assessments in an ongoing basis because DI builds upon a teacher's ability to correlate pre-assessment and post-assessment data to performance indicators and student learning profiles.[16] Performance assessment is a process by which individuals are required to perform an authentic task, rather than select an answer from a ready-made list or guess the best answer. Individuals develop personal approaches to the task under defined conditions, knowing that their work will be evaluated according to agreed-upon standards or previously established rubrics.

The significance of performance-based assessment has been anchored on the principle of reflective practice, which means that teachers are required to make the process of investigation, analysis, and problem solving an ongoing cycle in their practice, and not just reenact best practices.[17] Differentiation requires knowledge of both the instructional material and student characteristics, and the ability to establish meaningful interactions between the two.

To effectively implement differentiated instruction in the multicultural classroom, the twenty-first-century teacher needs to be familiar with certain concepts, issues, and practices that make differentiated instruction possible. These include knowledge of the skills and dispositions necessary for effective differentiation and knowledge of what is otherwise called multicultural proficiencies for the twenty-first-century classroom. They need to possess the foundational knowledge base of multicultural curriculum and teaching, and they need to be familiar with equity pedagogies.

MULTICULTURAL PROFICIENCIES FOR THE TWENTY-FIRST-CENTURY EDUCATION

There are certain knowledge bases, skills, and dispositions that teachers must possess to be able to teach in a multicultural classroom. These basic skills and competencies can be found in the Interstate Teacher Assessment and Support Consortium (InTASC) standards developed by Council of Chief State School Officers.[18] This is the same group that worked with the National Governors Association (NGA) to develop the Common Core State Standards (CCSS).

These standards were established to clearly identify what every teacher should know and be able to do to effectively prepare today's students for the twenty-first-century world of work and college readiness. These standards outline the common principles and foundations of teaching practice for all subject areas and grade levels, which are necessary for improving student achievement. These standards are built with insight from research and best practices on how all students learn.[19]

The standards that address multicultural proficiencies are addressed below:

- *Standard 1: Learner Development*. The teacher understands how learners grow and develop, recognizing that patterns of learning and development vary individually within and across the cognitive, linguistic, social, emotional, and physical areas, and designs and implements developmentally appropriate and challenging learning experiences.
- *Standard 2: Learning Differences*. The teacher uses understanding of individual differences and diverse cultures and communities to ensure inclusive learning environments that enable each learner to meet high standards.
- *Standard 3: Learning Environments*. The teacher works with others to create environments that support individual and collaborative learning and that encourage positive social interaction, active engagement in learning, and self-motivation.
- *Standard 4: Content Knowledge*. The teacher understands the central concepts, tools of inquiry, and structures of the discipline(s). He or she teaches and creates learning experiences that make the discipline accessible and meaningful for all learners to assure mastery of the content.
- *Standard 5: Application of Content*. The teacher understands how to connect concepts and use differing perspectives to engage learners in critical thinking, creativity, and collaborative problem solving related to authentic local and global issues.
- *Standard 6: Assessment*. The teacher understands and uses multiple methods of assessment to engage learners in their own growth, to monitor learners' progress, and to guide the teacher's and learner's decision making.
- *Standard 7: Planning for Instruction*. The teacher plans instruction that supports every student in meeting rigorous learning goals by drawing upon knowledge of content areas, curriculum, cross-disciplinary skills, and pedagogy, as well as knowledge of learners and the community context.
- *Standard 8: Instructional Strategies*. The teacher understands and uses a variety of instructional strategies to encourage learners to develop deep

understanding of content areas and their connections, and to build skills to apply knowledge in meaningful ways.
- *Standard 9: Professional Learning and Ethical Practice.* The teacher engages in ongoing professional learning and uses evidence to continually evaluate his or her practice, particularly the effects of his or her choices and actions on others (learners, families, other professionals, and the community), and adapts practice to meet the needs of each learner.
- *Standard 10: Leadership and Collaboration.* The teacher seeks appropriate leadership roles and opportunities to take responsibility for student learning, to collaborate with learners, families, colleagues, other school professionals, and community members to ensure learner growth, and to advance the profession.

Some states in the United States, like California, have articulated their own standards for the teaching profession. These standards often overlap in many areas with the InTASC standards. It is important that teachers become familiar with the teaching expectations and standards for teaching performance in their various states. Following California's lead, many states are now implementing Teacher Performance Assessments (TPAs), structured along standards for the teaching profession and aligned to address teacher expectations in meeting the Common Core State Standards in planning and teaching.

FOUNDATIONAL KNOWLEDGE BASE FOR MULTICULTURAL CURRICULUM AND TEACHING

According to Tiedt and Tiedt (2002), the scope and sequence of multicultural education ought to begin with the outcomes teachers expect their students to achieve. Some of the outcomes were identified as follows: increased students' self-esteem, understanding and appreciation of others, and a deepened concern for the needs of all people in the United States and the world.

To effectively differentiate in a multicultural classroom, contemporary teachers need to know about the following issues:

- Tracking—Teachers ought to know about America's history of tracking in education and work hard to reverse it.[20] This will ensure that we do not continue the bad history of tracking, which robbed many minority students of opportunities for academic success. Do not mistake it for differentiated instruction.
- Curriculum Knowledge—Multicultural teaching requires a deep knowledge of the educational curriculum, its foundational assumptions and phi-

losophies, and knowledge of alternative sources of information to provide balance to the existing curriculum. Teachers' subject matter knowledge is an indispensable ingredient in differentiation. Meaningful differentiation often calls for the teacher to go beyond the adopted textbook to secure materials that would make content comprehensible to students who need differentiation. A teacher must have a good grasp of his or her subject matter in order to know where to go to secure the relevant and appropriate material for supplementing the teaching resources.
- Knowledge of Students—Effective multicultural teaching demands a depth of knowledge of the students' cultures, history, and variety of experiences such as wealth, poverty, war experiences, health concerns, living conditions, and many other issues that affect who they are and how they learn. Effective teachers differentiate for students they know very well; they factor in their personal profile in articulating a relevant instructional program and create material to target their individual needs. They do not differentiate for generic students.
- Global Knowledge—An effective multicultural educator for the twenty-first-century classroom must possess a knowledge base beyond his or her local, regional, and national boundaries, to a global awareness that empowers him or her to speak to the changing dynamics of culture, history, politics, and other global issues of the day.

Issues on Equity Pedagogy and Multicultural Education

The basic argument underlying the idea of equity pedagogy is that with some modification in the way they plan and teach, teachers can significantly improve the academic achievement of students from diverse language, ethnic, racial, cultural, and socioeconomic backgrounds. Equity pedagogy confronts the problem of achievement gap, which has existed in the American educational system for many years.

The assumption behind equity pedagogy is that when minority students have access to qualified teachers with expertise in their fields, as well as knowledge of pedagogy and child development, they tend to perform better than otherwise.[21] Sheets (2005) proposed certain practices that would be classified as equity pedagogy:

- Use of multiple methods and approaches such as oral, written, performance-based activities, checklists, and anecdotal records
- Minimum competition in classroom interactions and more collaboration
- Application of assessment knowledge to the design, modification, and adaptation of learning events

- Use of assessment data to inform instruction
- Multiple opportunities for students to evaluate their own knowledge, skills, and abilities
- Promotion of "thinking about thinking" and the use of metacognitive strategies
- Teacher clarifying and modeling appropriate thinking and problem-solving strategies

Teacher Pedagogical Behaviors

The teacher has the role of facilitating the construction of students' knowledge by building a link between students' prior knowledge and new learning materials (Sheets 2005).[22] Sheets identified the following as relevant teacher behaviors that facilitate learning in the multicultural classroom:

- The teacher is able to identify and implement measurable goals for a diverse population of students in the content area.
- The teacher evaluates and adapts lessons to enhance students' understanding and mastery of the subject matter.
- The teacher recognizes and responds to student's perceptions, interpretations, or misconceptions to subject matter in a constructive way.
- The teacher is able to select content and strategies and uses a variety of styles to make them comprehensible.
- The teacher uses a variety of questioning strategies that encourage higher-order thinking and provides multiple opportunities to facilitate practice and mastery for students.

LESSON PLANNING FOR THE MULTICULTURAL CLASSROOM

Lesson planning in a multicultural classroom needs to depart from the exclusively traditional subject matter focus to a broader view of the need of the classroom community. The basic steps for preparing a lesson often vary from one teacher to the next and from one institution to another, yet the basic elements required remain the same.

There are seven steps that would be found in any standard lesson plan. Although the order may vary, the content remains the same: (1) goals and objectives, (2) materials and resources, (3) anticipatory set or entry, (4) instructional input, (5) guided practice, (6) independent practice, and (7) assessment/evaluation. Teacher is expected to check for understanding throughout the lesson. Using these steps, we will explore ways to integrate multicultural education into standards-based instructional planning and teaching.

Goals and Objectives

For a standards-based lesson plan in the state of California, for example, two basic tools are mandatory for teachers to familiarize themselves with: the goals should be derived from the California Common Core State Standards (CCSS) for mathematics and English language arts, the Next Generation Science Standards (NGSS), and the California Academic Content Standards for history, social studies, visual and performing arts, music, physical education, and other subjects not covered by the Common Core Standards. The standards provide the required learning and curriculum content needed in each content area for each grade level. These sources combine to make for a standards-based curriculum.

For a standards-based instruction, the standards remain the first point of call. Both Common Core State Standards and the State Academic Content Standards provide us with the broad and specific goals to be pursued in any lesson. Assume that a California art teacher wants to teach art critique and analysis to her seventh-grade class. Let's plan the lesson for her.

Goals and Standards Statement

The lesson is anchored on the seventh-grade California academic content standard for visual and performing arts, standard 4.0 (Aesthetic valuing), which reads, "Students analyze, assess, and derive meaning from works of art, including their own, according to the elements of art, the principles of design, and aesthetic qualities."

Let's narrow our focus down to substandard 4.2, which reads, "Analyze the form (how a work of art looks) and content (what a work of art communicates) of works of art." The standards provide us with the goal of the lesson, which specifies where this lesson is going, yet the teacher is required to isolate certain measurable objectives that would convince her at the end of this lesson that the destination was reached. This refers to the learning objectives.

Step 1: Learning Objectives

In a multicultural classroom, there is need for us to ensure that our objectives consider cognitive as well as affective domains of learning.[23] The objective is where the teacher articulates her expectations for students in relation to the stated goals, and it is also here that she articulates any multicultural and behavioral objective she wants to achieve through this lesson.

In keeping with Banks's third and fourth levels of multicultural education, the objectives here must not only be measurable, they must have transformational and social action focus. The task of the teacher is to teach a standards-based lesson, cleverly infusing multicultural education in such a way that students' worldviews are not only transformed, but they are led to do something to positively impact the world around them.

What is social action? someone may want to ask. Banks (2003) explains that

> [w]hen you identify concepts and generalizations, you should select those that will help students make decisions and take personal, social, or civic actions that reduce prejudice and discrimination in their personal lives, in the school, and, when possible, in the other social settings in which they function.[24]

Social action, therefore, is an action that is taken with the objective of enhancing the social status of another person or group of persons. Whatever thing we do to enhance the social status of another person or group is a social action. A social action objective, therefore, is an objective that aims at enhancing an individual's or group's social status.

In the case of this art lesson, this teacher may want to state the following academic objective: "Students will be able to create a collage of pictures representing the theme of homelessness and subsequently identify the thoughts and feelings associated with each art work." Homelessness is a social as well as multicultural issue, since it addresses a people's group within the larger society. The homeless represent marginal life and destitution. However, the objective does not contain any social action. Should the lesson end here, the academic goal would be fully met, but the multicultural impact will be very minimal.

To take it to the higher level, a second objective may need to be added: "After identifying the thoughts and feelings that those homeless scenes represent, students will list positive actions society can take to engage and mediate those feelings and thoughts, and the problem of homelessness in general."

The second objective brings in transformation, as students are led to critically engage the topic in question and propose solutions. However, there is no explicit social action yet. To bring in the social action part of the objective, let's add the following: "Students will hold an exhibition of their art work on homelessness and the suggested strategies that can be used in addressing it. This may assist people to begin to adjust their attitudes toward the homeless." Thus a simple art lesson can produce a change of attitude and a changed society. This is social action.

The goal and objectives of a lesson may be considered the most crucial part, as time needs to be spent articulating its academic and social objectives and merging them in one lesson plan. One of the areas teachers may face challenges is articulating a valid social action for primary-grade students. In responding to this challenge, Banks argues, "Primary grade students cannot take actions that will reduce discrimination in the larger society. However, they can make a commitment to not tell or laugh at racist jokes, to play with and make friends with students from other racial, ethnic, religious groups."[24]

Banks seems to have a narrow view of social action in submitting that primary grades "cannot take social actions." Social action can be undertaken at any grade level. Choosing not to tell or laugh at racist jokes is an action. Primary-grade students have been known to undertake fund-raising to help the poor and homeless, so they can do social action.

According to Taylor and Whittaker (2003), "[O]nce the major goal for implementing a change process have been chosen and prioritized, the steps for achieving these goals must be delineated."[25] According to them, a plan of action may involve reference to the time and place of the action, like the next classroom, assembly ground, community, or neighborhood. This specific detail is not expected to be part of the objectives statement. It is usually best presented as part of the independent practice (step 6). Moving on from goals and objectives, let's go to the next level.

Step 2: Materials Needed

The materials that will be needed for this lesson would include poster boards, magazines and newspapers (which will have pictures of the homeless from across all gender and ethnicities), glue sticks, markers, pens and pencils, and paper.

Step 3: Anticipatory Set or Entry

This step is often called "entry" as it excites, arouses interest in, and prepares the students for the learning experience. A good reading that can accomplish these for this lesson and provoke student curiosity about the homeless or art appreciation can be selected. Kathleen Krull's *Lives of the Artists: Masterpieces, Messes (and What the Neighbors Thought)* could make a good anticipatory set. The story is read and briefly discussed, and the teacher quickly transitions into the lesson. Another form of art anticipatory set may be to preview the lesson by checking what the students already know on the topic so as to avoid repeating what they already know.

One good way is to use the KWL chart. This chart asks students for what they already know on the subject (K), what they want to know about the subject (W), and what they have learned (L). The good thing about the KWL chart is that it serves as an anticipatory set, a scaffold for introducing new ideas, and as a way to summarize and assess learning. In this case, students can tell what they already know about collages, the homeless, and more. They can state what they want to learn about each of the concepts to be addressed. At the end they will summarize what they learned in terms of art analysis and critique, as well as the homeless.

Step 4: Instructional Input

This is the place the teacher presents and explains basic concepts, definitions, and clarifications students need to comprehend the lesson. Here is where new concepts are introduced. According to Barba (1998), decisions about your instructional strategies need to depend on the characteristics of your students, information to be learned, and your goals and objectives. This is the right place to specify what scaffolds you intend to use in delivering instruction to special needs students or English learners, as you plan.

For this lesson, the teacher will need to define and explain such words as *collage*, *homelessness*, and *aesthetic valuing*. Word study (along with pictures) may be additional scaffolds for students who are English learners. The teacher will need to present a variety of collages for illustration. She needs to explain to students how pulling together different shapes and forms that were otherwise unrelated created the collages. She could separate the various parts of a collage to demonstrate to students what a collage means and how they are formed.

She can then demonstrate the process involved in making collages by starting a collage from scratch and finishing it as students watch. This is called *modeling*. After the demonstration, the first part of her direct instruction has ended.

Step 5: Guided Practice

Here, she hands the students a set of arts activity materials containing blank paper and clippings from various magazines. Each student would have the same set of items. She will then lead them to make a collage giving them step-by-step direction.

The instructions on the activity can also be typed up and given to individual students. The teacher walks around making sure everyone is following her instruction. She ensures that each step is clear and comprehensible to everyone. When everyone has completed that task, she is ready to discuss. She leads them through a discussion of the art principles (form and content) as well as social/multicultural issues represented by their collages. She models for them how to analyze a piece of art and how to decipher their hidden messages. She models all these for the students; that way the whole process is clear to them.

Given the fact that homelessness presents the object of analysis and critique, a discussion of the hidden messages in the art piece would reveal the plight of the homeless and the social questions it would provoke. This way, the discussion of the multicultural objectives of this course is not pursued outside of the scope of the lesson's academic goals and objectives—form and content of art.

Step 6: Independent Practice

At this point, the students have fully experienced the process of making collages as well as deciphering the hidden messages through analysis and critique. They have also discussed the social implications of the feeling aroused by homelessness and how the art pieces portray them. Now they are going to create their own unique collages of the homeless and use them to communicate unique messages about homelessness.

It will be the task of classmates to decipher the message contained in other classmates' artwork as they work in pairs or small groups to analyze their works. Part of the independent practice may be to work individually or in small groups to produce collages that would present positive ways to respond to the feelings and faces of hopelessness in the homeless.

It could also be a written piece that analyzes the feelings and thoughts. The two pieces of work can then be presented to the public (which could be school community, school bulletin board, open-house day, community center, etc.) for viewing. Now social action is completed. The multicultural message has been communicated outside the classroom.

Step 7: Assessment and Evaluation

At this point, the teacher may choose to require a written analysis of at least one piece of art from each student. Each assessment may be placed next to the artist's own piece of communicative intent, and the success may depend on how closely the critic comes to the artist's communicative intent. The evaluation may also be anchored on the exhibition. Written comments can be solicited from viewers and such comments would indicate whether the artists were successful in presenting the two views of homelessness through their works of art or not.

Lesson Extension

Extending the lesson beyond visual and performing arts, a language art lesson can be developed for the same seventh-grade classroom with a good multicultural twist on the following goals and objectives:

Step One: Goals and Objective

Standard: Write informative/explanatory texts to examine a topic and convey ideas, concepts, and information through the selection, organization, and analysis of relevant content—California 7th Grade Common Core State Standards for English Language Arts, for writing (Standard 2 a-e).

Objective: Students will identify and write a short essay on homelessness after reading the story "Bums in the Attic" from the book *The House on Mango Street*.

Social Action: Students will go to neighborhood grocery stores and solicit enough supplies to make 101 lunches for the homeless. The supplies will be donated to a homeless shelter.

QUESTIONS AND APPLICATION

Case Study

Norton Elementary School in South Hollywood was committed to educating their students about cultural diversity. They have always celebrated the cultural holidays in a big way. This year the plan was to celebrate Cinco de Mayo in a special way. They invited a folklorico dance group from Baja California who came to the school and performed during a special assembly for the occasion. Students and teachers had a great time dancing and interacting with the special dance group with which most of them were unfamiliar.

The Challenge

During this special assembly, no attempt was made to explain to the students and the audience of interested parents what Cinco de Mayo celebration was all about. No attempt was made to explain the history and significance of the Folklorico dance in the Mexican culture. No attempt was made to address the issue of Mexican immigration challenges in the United States either—at the assembly or in the classrooms. Apart from the entertainment from the performance, nothing was done to highlight the values and challenges the Mexican culture presents to the United States.

Follow-Up Questions

a. What level of multicultural education would you say the activity represented?

b. What are the different ways the Folklorico group could have been utilized to make multicultural education more in-depth and possibly reach the transformation and social action levels at this school?
c. What other activities could have been carried out at this school that would have been more effective than inviting the Folklorico group?

Review Questions

a. Describe the four levels of multicultural education by James Banks.
b. Compare and contrast the transformation level and the social action level.
c. Define a social action objective. Distinguish a social action objective from a regular academic objective.
d. Select any standard lesson from either the internet or other source and articulate a social action objective that can fit that lesson.

STRATEGIES FOR APPLICATION IN THE K–12 CLASSROOMS

Here are some social action projects that can be used across disciplines and grade levels in the K–12 classrooms:

1. *Grades 7–12*: Lessons on discrimination. Students can write papers or make collages of actions that can be taken to engage discrimination and display them in conspicuous places at the school.
2. *Grades K–12*: Students can develop plans for peaceful engagement of a current social problem. The entire class can implement the plan.
3. *Grades 4–12*: Language arts, Spanish language, or history/social studies lessons. Students can research biographies of Latinos and Latino Americans, African Americans, Jews, and other non–Western Europeans. Each student can create a pictorial biography of one of the characters studied. The class work can be posted on the school bulletin board.
4. *Grades 7–12*: A physical education lesson on soccer can focus on the HIV/AIDS issue in Brazil or Africa, homes of the game of soccer, and engage students to become actively involved in combating this disease.
5. *Grades K–12*: A language arts lesson can use the story of Jackie Robinson as its context either for reading comprehension, literary analysis, or other forms of language arts activities. This will provide the forum for discussing discrimination. Students can write papers, draw pictures, or make posters on their personal experiences of unfair treatment: being picked last in a game or being left out altogether.

6. *Grades 9–11*: A language arts lesson can focus on an analysis of recent court rulings involving civil rights, such as a recent U.S. Supreme Court ruling that strengthened and expanded the rights of cities and counties to enforce the "eminent domain" laws. The class can discuss these rulings and use notes from their discussions to write an open letter to their city, county, or state leaders expressing their personal opinions on those rulings.

Notes

CHAPTER 1

1. J. Cornelius-White. 2007. "Learner-Centered Teacher-Student Relationships Are Effective: A Meta-Analysis." *Review of Educational Research* 77, 113–43; K. L. Brown. 2003. "From Teacher-Centered to Learner-Centered Curriculum: Improving Learning in Diverse Classrooms." *Education* 124, 49–54; R. D. Crick and B. L. McCombs. 2006. "The Assessment of Learner-Centered Practices Surveys: An English Case Study." *Educational Research and Evaluation* 12, 423–44; M. Harris and R. Cullen. 2008. "Learner-Centered Leadership: An Agenda for Action." *Innovation in Higher Education* 33, 21–28.

2. J. Ashton and L. Newman. 2006. "An Unfinished Symphony: 21st Century Teacher Education Using Knowledge Creating Heutagogies." *British Journal of Educational Technology* 37, no. 6, 825–40.

3. P. O. Ozuah. 2005. "First, There Was Pedagogy and Then Came Andragogy." *Einstein Journal of Biology and Medicine* 21, no. 2, 83–87.

4. J. Ashton and L. Newman 2006.

5. S. Chan. 2010. "Applications of Andragogy in Multi-Disciplined Teaching and Learning." *Journal of Adult Education* 39, no. 2, 25–35.

6. J. Ashton and L. Newman 2006.

7. A. Ryan. 1998. "Deweyan Pragmatism and the American Education." In *Philosophers on Education*, ed. A. O. Rorty (New York: Routledge).

8. Adapted from Chan 2010; B. Taylor and M. Kroth. 2009. "A Single Conversation with a Wise Man Is Better Than Ten Years of Study: A Model for Testing Methodologies for Pedagogy or Andragogy." *Journal of the Scholarship of Teaching and Learning* 9, no. 2, 42–56.

9. J. Ashton and L. Newman 2006.

10. C. Kenyon and S. Hase. 2001. "Moving from Andragogy to Hetuagogy in Vocational Education." In *Research to Reality: Putting VET Research to Work*. Proceedings

of the Australian Vocational Education and Training Research Association (AVETRA) conference, Adelaide, Australia, March 28–30.

11. *Webster's New Twentieth Century Dictionary of English Language*, 1968, p. 576.

12. B. F. Skinner. 1968. *The Technology of Teaching* (New York: Meredith Corporation), 3.

13. R. P. Hawkins. 1990. "The Life and Contributions of Burrhus Frederick Skinner." *Education and Treatment of Children* 13, no. 3, 258–63.

14. B. F. Skinner 1968, 3.

15. B. F. Skinner 1968, 3.

16. B. F. Skinner 1968, 2–3.

17. D. R. Weinberg. 2011. "Montessori, Maslow, and Self-Actualization." *Montessori Life* (Winter 2011–2012), 16–21.

18. A. Maslow. 1968. *Toward a Psychology of Being* (New York: Van Nostrand Reinhold).

19. Within the educational contexts you construct knowledge, personalities, and social arrangements. Education shapes and molds the lives that shape and mold society.

CHAPTER 2

1. Communication Theory. 2017. "Cultural Identity Theory." Retrieved from http://communicationtheory.org/cultural-identity-theory/; Y. Chen and H. Lin. 2016. "Cultural Identities." Communication Oxford Research Encyclopaedias. Retrieved from http://communication.oxfordre.com/view/10.1093/acrefore/9780190228613.001.0001/acrefore-9780190228613-e-20.

2. N. M. Ford. 1988. *When Did I Begin? Conception of the Human Individual in History, Philosophy and Science* (New York: Cambridge University Press).

3. H. Titus. 1970. *Living Issues in Philosophy* (New York: Van Nostrand Reinhold Company), 130; H. Titus. 1995. *Living Issues in Philosophy*, 9th ed. (Belmont, CA: Wadsworth).

4. Titus 1970, 131–32.

5. Titus 1970.

6. Titus 1970, 134; A. Reichenbach. (2016). "Human Skulls Found in Schuylkill County." Retrieved from http://wkok.com/human-skull-found-in-schuylkill-county/.

7. Titus, 156.

8. The idea of family in America today has been expanded to include many different expressions of domestic partnership: Two males with children, two females with children, grandparent(s) with grandchildren, even foster homes and more, in addition to the traditional mother and father with children.

9. A. Mile. 2014. "Addressing the Problem of Cultural Anchoring: An Identity-Based Model of Culture in Action." *Social Psychology Quarterly* 77, no. 2, 210–27.

10. J. J. Romo, P. Bradfield, and R. Serrano. 2004. *Reclaiming Democracy: Multicultural Educators' Journeys toward Transformative Teaching* (Upper Saddle River, NJ: Pearson Education).

CHAPTER 3

1. A. L. Kroeber and C. Kluckhohn. 1952. *Culture: A Critical Review of Concepts and Definitions*, with W. Untereiner and appendices by Alfred G. Meyer (Cambridge, MA: The Museum), 357.

2. Kroeber and Kluckhohn 1952, 357.

3. This American image may be acting against American interest in certain circles as other nationalities have often come to interpret this as arrogance and inability to be considerate of others. A fellow professor from Toronto University commented that American tourists in Canada had impressed upon her this negative image, and it would be difficult to convince her otherwise.

4. On September 11, 2001, the World Trade Center building in New York City was destroyed by Arab Muslim terrorists who had hijacked airplanes and flew into it. They also attacked the U.S. Defense Headquarters (the Pentagon) and attempted attacks on other sites, including the White House.

5. The U.S. Declaration of Independence declares, "All men are created equal and endowed with such inalienable rights as life, liberty, and the pursuit of happiness." The pursuit of happiness, like the other two, have become a fundamental aspect of the American lifestyle.

6. D. M. Gollnick and P. C. Chinn. 2009. *Multicultural Education in a Pluralistic Society* (Upper Saddle River, NJ: Pearson Education).

7. C. Kraft. 1979. *Christianity in Culture* (Maryknoll, NY: Orbis Books).

8. H. L. Tischler, P. Whitten, and D. E. K. Hunter. 1986. *Introduction to Sociology* (New York: CBS College Publishing).

9. Tischler, Whitten, and Hunter 1986, 145.

10. Ibid.

11. E. Durkheim. 1915. *The Elementary Forms of Religious Life: A Study of Religious Sociology* (New York: Macmillan).

12. Tischler, Whitten, and Hunter 1986, 460.

13. The Declaration of Independence (1776).

14. A. Lincoln. 1863. Address made at Gettysburg, Pennsylvania, November 19, 1863.

15. W. O. Kellog. 1995. *American History: The Easy Way* (New York: Barron's Educational Series).

16. P. Gorski. 2004. "Multicultural Pavilion." Retrieved from http://www.edchange.org/multicultural, accessed on October 8, 2007; R. Frank. (2016). "Record Number of Millionaires Living in the U.S." Retrieved from http://www.cnbc.com/2016/03/07/record-number-of-millionaires-living-in-the-us.html; Knoema. 2016. "Wealth of the World's Richest People vs. GDP of Countries." Retrieved from https://knoema.com/infographics/wqezguc/wealth-of-the-world-s-richest-people-vs-gdp-of-countries.

17. A. Toffler. 1990. *Powershift: Knowledge, Wealth, and Violence at the Edge of the 21st Century* (New York: Bantam Books), 20 (cf. Russell Chandler [1992], 45). (Emphasis added.)

18. Gorski 2004; Internet World Stats. 2016. "Top 20 Countries with the Highest Internet Users." Retrieved from http://www.internetworldstats.com/top20.htm.

19. J. O. Hertzler. 1946. *Social Institutions* (Lincoln, NE: University of Nebraska Press).

20. T. E. Lasswell, J. H. Burma, and S. H. Aronson (eds.). 1970. *Life in Society: Readings in Sociology* (Glenview, IL: Scott, Foresman and Company).

21. Cf. U.S. Census Bureau, U.S. Department of Justice, U.S. Office of Management and Budget; http://www.edchange.org/multicultural.

22. Gorski 2004.

23. Kraft 1979, 53.

24. A. Etzioni. 1968. *The Active Society: A Theory of Societal and Political Processes* (New York: Free Press), 13–14.

25. M. Weber. 1958. *The Protestant Ethic and the Spirit of Capitalism.* Translated by Talcott Parsons (New York: Charles Scribner's Sons).

26. In Weber's analysis of Benjamin Franklin's view of money, he indicated that Franklin considered a lack of care in handling money as tantamount to murdering capital embryos and was an ethical defect on the side of the culprit (cf. Weber 1958, 196).

27. R. P. Cuzzort and E. W. King. 1976. *Humanity and Modern Social Thought* (Hinsdale, IL: Dryden Press), 48.

28. P. Schaff. 1888. *History of the Christian Church* (Peabody, MA: Hendrickson Publishing), 221.

29. Cuzzort and King 1976, 49.

30. Gorski 2004.

31. R. A. Nisbet. 1965. *Emile Durkheim* (Westport, CT: Greenwood Press).

CHAPTER 4

1. K. Koppelman and R. L. Goodhart. 2005. *Understanding Human Differences: Multicultural Education for Diverse America* (Boston: Pearson Education).

2. Cf. D. Lindsay, ed. (n.d.). *Abraham Lincoln/Jefferson Davis: A House Divided* (Cleveland, OH: Howard Allen).

3. J. Kozol. 2005. *The Shame of the Nation: The Restoration of Apartheid Schooling in America* (New York: Crown Publishers).

4. J. Levin and W. Levin. 1982. *The Functions of Discrimination and Prejudice*, 2nd ed. (New York: Harper & Row).

5. S. Covey. 1986. *The Seven Habits of Highly Effective People* (Gahanna, OH: Covey Leadership Center).

6. L. Raths, M. Harmin, and S. Simon. 1966. *Values and Teaching: Working with Values in the Classroom* (Columbus, OH: Charles E. Merrill).

7. R. Hernandez-Sheets. 2009. "What Is Diversity Pedagogy?" *Multicultural Education* 16, no. 3, 11–17.

8. R. Lindsey, K. N. Robins, and R. D. Terrell. 1999. *Cultural Proficiency: A Manual for School Leaders* (Thousand Oaks, CA: Corwin); R. Lindsey, L. M. Roberts, and F. Campbell Jones. 2005. *The Culturally Proficient School: An Implementation Guide for School Leaders* (Thousand Oaks, CA: Corwin).

9. A 1993–1994 U.S. Department of Education, National Center for Educational Statistics, School Staffing Survey reported the percentage of public school teachers who are white, non-Hispanic, as between 84 percent and 87 percent (cf. http://nces.ed.gov/pubs97/97460.pdf).

10. This certification was renamed the California Teachers of English Learners (CTEL).

11. L. Derman-Sparks. 1993. *Anti-Bias Curriculum: Tools for Empowering Young Children* (Washington, DC: Author).

12. G. Allport. 1954. *The Nature of Prejudice* (Reading, MA: Addison-Wesley).

13. M. L. Weymeyer and M. Schwartz. 2001. "Disproportionate Representation of Males in Special Education Services: Biology, Behavior, or Bias?" *Education and Treatment of Children* 24, no. 1, 28–45.

14. C. W. Cooper. 2003. "The Detrimental Impact of Teacher Bias: Lessons Learned from Standpoint of African American Mothers." *Teachers Education Quarterly* 30, no. 2 (Spring), 101–14. (Cf. Bartolome 1994; Cochran-Smith 1997; Fueyo and Betchtol 1999; Oakes and Lipton 1999).

15. G. Ladson-Billings. 1995. "But That's Just Good Teaching! The Case for Culturally Relevant Pedagogy." *Theory into Practice* 34, no. 3, 159–65.

16. Personal Communication.

17. L. T. Diaz-Rico and K. Z. Weed. 1995. *The Cross-Cultural, Language, and Academic Development Handbook: A Study in Religious Sociology* (New York: Macmillan).

18. E. P. Cubberly. 1909. *Changing Conceptions of Education* (Boston: Houghton Mifflin).

19. American cultural pluralism covers ethnic and religious diversities.

20. Indeed, the ideal picture of America may not be the Congress in session but rather the U.S. military, with white soldiers, African-American soldiers, Hispanic soldiers, Asian soldiers, and so on, each pointing a gun, not at each other, but to a common enemy.

21. J. M. Jones. 1997. *Prejudice and Racism* (New York: McGraw-Hill).

22. K. Cockley. 2002. "Testing Cross's Revised Racial Identity Model: An Examination of the Relationship between Racial Identity and Internalized Racialism." *Journal of Counseling Psychology* 49, no. 4, 476–83.

23. Cf. California Newsreel. 2003. *Race: The Power of an Illusion*, a motion picture production by the Public Broadcasting Service (PBS).

24. J. Kozol. 1991. *Savage Inequalities: Children in America's Schools* (New York: Crown Publishers).

CHAPTER 5

1. J. A. Banks. 2004. *Handbook of Research on Multicultural Education*, 2nd ed., edited by J. A. Banks and C. A. M. Banks (San Francisco: John Wiley & Sons), 3.

2. The U.S. Declaration of Independence states that all men are created equal and endowed with certain inalienable human rights. The right to equal treatment in educational opportunity has been viewed as a civil right by many.

3. It was June 7, 1892, when a shoemaker by the name of Homer Plessy, defined as "one-eighth black and seven-eighths white" was jailed for sitting in the "white" car of the East Louisiana Railroad. He went to court to argue that the separate car violated his Thirteenth and Fourteenth Amendment rights. The judge in the case, John Howard Ferguson, ruled that the state of Louisiana had the right to regulate different cars for different peoples for railroads operating in the state. In so ruling, he found Plessy guilty of refusing to leave the white car. A U.S. Supreme Court upheld this decision in 1896.

4. M. J. Klarman. 2004. *From Jim Crow to Civil Rights: The Supreme Court and the Struggle for Racial Equality* (New York: Oxford University Press); P. Irons. 2002. *Jim Crow's Children: The Broken Promise of the Brown Decision* (New York: Penguin).

5. This federal law, which was proposed by Senator Charles Sumner, a Republican congressman, guaranteed every American regardless of race, color, or previous conditions of servitude the same treatment in public accommodations (including transportation and access to public places).

6. This law declared all rail companies in Louisiana must provide separate but equal accommodations for white and non-white passengers. The penalty for sitting in the wrong car was $25 or twenty days in jail.

7. *Plessy v. Ferguson*, 163 U.S. 537 [1896].

8. *Plessy v. Ferguson*, 163 U.S. 537 [1896].

9. *Plessy v. Ferguson*, 163 U.S. 537 [1896].

10. M. W. La Morte. 1999. *School Law: Cases and Concepts* (Boston, MA: Allyn and Bacon), 272.

11. R. J. Cottrol, R. T. Diamone, and L. B. Ware. 2003. *Brown v. Board of Education: Caste, Culture, and the Constitution* (Kansas: University Press of Kansas), 128–29. M. J. Klarman. 2007. *Brown v. Board of Education and the Civil Rights Movement* (New York: Oxford University Press), 55–58.

12. *Brown v. Board of Education*, 347 U.S. 483 [1954].

13. 347 U.S. 483 [1954].

14. 347 U.S. 483 [1954].

15. 347 U.S. 483 [1954].

16. M. W. La Morte. 1999. *School Law: Cases and Concepts* (Boston, MA: Allyn and Bacon), 356; M. W. La Morte. 2011. *School Law: Cases and Concepts* (Boston, MA: Allyn and Bacon).

17. *Lau v. Nichols*, 414 U.S. 563 [1974]. Retrieved from http://supct.law.cornell.edu, accessed on March 30, 2005.

18. U.S. Constitution, 1868.

19. *Brown v. Board of Education*, 347 U.S. 483 [1954].

20. This book documents the most shocking stories about the deplorable conditions under which America's poor and mostly minority students are subjected in the name of schooling.

21. J. Kozol. 1991. *Savage Inequalities: Children in America's Schools* (New York: Crown Publishers).

22. No Child Left Behind (NCLB) was enacted in 2001 by President George W. Bush toward better accountability and improved student achievement.

23. G. Gay. 2004. "Educational Equality for Students of Color." In *Multicultural Education: Issues and Perspectives* by J. A. Banks and C. A. McGee-Banks (New York: John Wiley & Sons), 228.

24. J. A. Banks 2004, 19.

CHAPTER 6

1. H. Nagai. 2002. "Multicultural Education in the United States and Japan." Paper presented at the 46th Annual Conference of Comparative International Education Society (CIES), Orlando, Florida, March 6–8.

2. J. A. Banks. 2003. "Multicultural Education: Characteristics and Goals." In *Multicultural Education: Issues and Perspectives*, 4th ed. Edited by J. A. Banks and C. A. McGee-Banks (New York: John Wiley & Sons, Inc.).

3. D. Sadkler and M. Sadkler. 1994. *Teachers, Schools and Society* (Princeton, NJ: McGraw-Hill).

4. Horace Mann is regarded as one of the individuals who shaped the American educational landscape. He is often referred to as the "Father of American Education." He became the U.S. secretary of education and used that opportunity to sell his vision of education as part of the birthright of every American child. He referred to education as the "great equalizer."

5. J. E. Hernandez-Tutop. 1998. "Oppressor: The Educational System." Opinion Paper published by the U.S. Department of Education, p. 3.

6. R. Ueda. 1993. "The Construction of Ethnic Diversity and National Identity in the Public Schools." In *Historical Perspectives on the Current Education Reforms*. Edited by Diane Ravitch and Maris Vinovskis. Essays commissioned by the Office of Research (OR) in the Office of the Educational Research and Improvement (OERI), U.S. Department of Education.

7. Cf. N. V. Montalto. 1982. *A History of the Intercultural Educational Movement, 1924–1941* (New York: Garland).

8. Jim Crow laws are a series of laws that established a racial caste system primarily, but not exclusively, in the Southern and border states between 1876 and the 1960s. These series of laws legitimized segregation against blacks and other minorities and became the basis on which anti-black sentiments spread across the United States. Individuals that once lived alongside their black slaves in harmony became so hostile to these now freed people that they would not share a restaurant, drinking fountain, railcar, or other public facilities with them. It is the law that also launched a series of lynchings that marked the darkest period of the black experience in the United States.

9. http://www.ferris.edu/news/jimcrow/origins.htm.

10. J. A. Banks 2004.

11. Williams is said to have been born in Bedford Springs, Pennsylvania, on October 16, 1849, and died in Blackpool, England, August 1891. He is credited with writing the first objective and scientifically researched history of African Americans. His works include *History of the Negro Race in America From 1619 to 1880* (1882), and *A History of Negro Troops in the War of Rebellion*.

12. G. Nash. 1993. "Multiculturalism and History: Historical Perspectives and Present Prospects." In *Historical Perspectives on the Current Education Reforms*. Edited by Diane Ravitch and Maris Vinovskis. Essays commissioned by the Office of Research (OR) in the Office of Educational Research and Improvement (OERI), U.S. Department of Education.

13. J. A. Banks 2004.

14. Cf. Oakes 1985; Valenzuela 1999; Mehan, Villanueva, Hubbad, and Lintz 1996; Yonezawa, Wells, and Serna 2002.

15. D. Kirp. 1993. "The Educational Equities in Historical Perspective." In *Historical Perspectives on the Current Education Reforms*. Edited by Diane Ravitch and Maris Vinovskis. Essays commissioned by the Office of Research (OR) in the Office of Educational Research and Improvement (OERI), U.S. Department of Education.

16. J. Weiler. 1998. "Recent Changes in School Desegregation." ERIC/CUE Digest Number 133. Cf. H. D. Willis. 1994 (November 1). "The Shifting Focus in School Desegregation." Paper presented to the SWRL board of directors and the 1995 Equity Conference.

17. *Plessey v. Ferguson*, 163 U.S. 537 [1896].

18. *Brown v. Board of Education*, 347 U.S. 483 [1954] [USSC+].

19. Rosa Parks has been labeled the "mother of the modern civil rights movement" in America. Her refusal to move was done at the risk of legal sanctions as well as physical harm, yet that deliberate act of defiance sparked the fire that led to the modern civil rights movement.

20. B. Brunner and E. Haney. n.d. "Civil Rights Timeline: Milestones in the Modern Civil Rights Movement." Accessed on October 9, 2006, from http://www.infoplease.com/spot/civilrightstimeline1.html.

21. Brunner and Haney (n.d.).

22. R. Moses and C. E. Cobb Jr. 2001. *Radical Equations: Math Literacy and Civil Rights* (Boston: Beacon Press).

23. J. A. Banks 2004.

24. C. G. Woodson and C. H. Wesley. 1922. *The Negro in Our History* (Washington, DC: Associated Publishers).

25. W. E. B. Du Bois. 1935. *Black Reconstruction* (New York: Harcourt Brace).

26. G. Nash. 1993. "Multiculturalism and History: Historical Perspectives and Present Prospects." In *Historical Perspectives on the Current Education Reforms*. Edited by Diane Ravitch and Maris Vinovskis. Essays commissioned by the Office of Research (OR) in the Office of Educational Research and Improvement (OERI), U.S. Department of Education.

27. Cf. J. D. Pulliam and J. J. Van Patten. 2003. *History of Education in America* (Upper Saddle River, NJ: Pearson Education).

28. M. F. Suleiman. 1996. "Preparing Teachers for the Culturally Diverse Classrooms." Paper presented at the 7th Annual Effective Schools Conference (Topeka, Kansas: May 3–5).

29. *Brown v. Board of Education*, 347 U.S. 483 [1954] [USSC+].

30. U.S. Equal Employment Opportunities Commission. 1964. Title VII of the Civil Rights Act of 1964. Retrieved from https://www.eeoc.gov/laws/statutes/title vii.cfm.

31. U.S. Department of Education. 1974. Equal Educational Opportunities Act (EEOA). Retrieved from https://www.congress.gov/bill/93rd-congress/house-bill/40.

32. J. A. Banks 2004.

33. Banks and Banks 2005.

34. K. Maclay. 2003. "Anthropology Professor John Ogbu Dies at Age 64." Accessed on October 7, 2006, from http://www.berkeley.edu/news/media/releases/2003/08/26_ogbu.shtml.

35. List is taken from http://www.berkeley.edu/news/media/releases/2003/08/26_ogbu.shtml.

36. G. J. Conti. 1977. "Rebels with a Cause: Myles Horton and Paulo Friere." *Community College Review* 5, no. 1, 36–43.

37. P. Friere. 1998. "Cultural Action and Conscientization." *Harvard Educational Review* 68, no. 4, 505.

38. Friere 1998, 505.

39. Conti 1977.

40. C. Sleeter, M. N. Torres, and P. Laughlin. 2004. "Scaffolding Conscientization through Inquiry in Teacher Education." *Teacher Education Quarterly* 31, no. 1, 81–96.

41. B. Wade. 1998. "Introduction: Literacy and Schooling." *Educational Review* 50, no. 2, 103–4.

42. E. Friedland. 2004. "Education for Liberation: Making the Classroom a Place for Thinking and Creating." *Multicultural Education* 12, no. 2, 2–7.

43. The most significant impact of Elliott's campaign is her insistence that one person can make a difference.

CHAPTER 7

1. S. Thompson. 2001. "The Authentic Standards Movement and Its Evil Twin." *Phi Delta Kappan* 82, no. 5, 358.

2. Thompson 2001, 358.

3. E. G. Cohen. 1984. "Talking and Working Together: Status, Interactions, and Learning." In P. L. Peterson, L. C. Wilkerson, and M. Hallinan (eds.), *The Social Context of Instruction: Group Organization and Group Process* (New York: Academic Press), 171–87.

4. J. Wang and S. J. Odell. 2002. "Mentored Learning to Teach according to Standards-Based Reform: A Critical Review." *Review of Educational Research* 72, no. 3, 481–546.

5. B. Falk. 2002. "Standards-Based Reforms: Problems and Possibilities." *Phi Delta Kappan* 83, no. 8, 612–20.

6. Edsource. 2003 (September/October). "Standards in Focus." *Leadership* 33, no. 1, 28–31.

7. M. Chatterji. 2002. "Models and Methods for Examining Standards-Based Reforms and Accountability Initiatives: Have the Tools of Inquiry Answered Pressing Questions on Improving Schools?" *Review of Educational Research* 72, no. 3, 345–86.

8. Banks 2003, 250.

9. Banks 2003, 235.

10. Banks 2003, 229.

11. L. Salazar, C. A. Falkenberg, S. Nullman, M. C. Silio, and A. Nevin. 2004. "Universal Design and Differentiated Instruction: A Position Paper to Resolve Potentially Competing Mandates of the Individuals with Disabilities Education Act and No Child Left Behind." Submitted to *Resources in Education*.

12. C. A. Tomlinson. 2000. "Differentiation of Instruction in the Elementary Grades." ERIC Digest.

13. S. Keck and S. C. Kinney. 2005 (September). "Creating a Differentiated Classroom." *Learning and Leading with Technology*.

14. C. A. Tomlinson. 1999. *Differentiated Classroom: Responding to the Need of All Learners* (Alexandria, VA: Virginia Association of Supervision and Curriculum Development).

15. C. A. Tomlinson. 1995. *How to Differentiate Instruction in Mixed-Ability Classrooms* (Alexandria, VA: Association for Supervision and Curriculum Development).

16. C. V. Parsons and J. M. DeLucia. 2005 (September). "Decision Making in the Process of Differentiation." *Learning and Leading with Technology*.

17. R. R. Chung. 2008. "Beyond Assessment: Performance Assessments in Teacher Education." *Teacher Education Quarterly* 35, no. 1, 7–28; L. Shulman. 1987. "Knowledge and Teaching: Foundations of the New Reform." *Harvard Educational Review* 57, no. 1, 1–22; D. A. Schon. 1983. *The Reflective Practitioner: How Professionals Think in Action* (New York: Basic Books).

18. Council of Chief State School Officers (CCSSO). 2011 (April). *Interstate Teacher Assessment and Support Consortium (InTASC) Model Core Teaching Standards: A Resource for State Dialogue* (Washington, DC: Author).

19. CCSSO 2011.

20. S. Nieto and P. Bode. 2012. *Affirming Diversity: The Sociopolitical Context of Multicultural Education.* 6th. ed. (Boston: Pearson), 110–12.

21. J. Banks. 2006. *Cultural Diversity and Education: Foundations, Curriculum, and Teaching* (Boston: Pearson Education), 15.

22. R. H. Sheets. 2005. *Diversity Pedagogy: Examining the Role of Culture in the Teaching-Learning Process* (Boston: Pearson Education).

23. Banks 2003, 109.

24. Banks 2003, 108.

25. Taylor and Whittaker 2003, 76.

References

Allport, G. 1954. *The Nature of Prejudice.* Reading, MA: Addison-Wesley Publishing.

Ashton, J., and L. Newman. 2006. "An Unfinished Symphony: 21st Century Teacher Education Using Knowledge Creating Heutagogies." *British Journal of Educational Technology* 37 (6): 825–40.

Banks, J. A. 2003. "Multicultural Education: Characteristics and Goals." In J. A. Banks and C. A. M. Banks (Eds.), *Multicultural Education: Issues and Perspectives* (4th ed.). New York: John Wiley & Sons.

Banks, J. A. 2003. *Multicultural Education: Issues and Perspectives* (4th ed., rev.), by J. A. Banks and C. A. M. Banks (Eds.). New York: John Wiley & Sons.

Banks, J. A. 2003. *Teaching Strategies for Ethnic Studies* (7th ed.). Boston: Allyn & Bacon.

Banks, J. A. 2003. *Teaching Strategies for Ethnic Studies.* Boston: Pearson Education Group, Inc.

Banks, J. A. 2004. *Handbook of Research on Multicultural Education* (2nd ed.), J. A. Banks & C. A. M. Banks (Eds.). San Francisco: John Wiley & Sons.

Banks, J. 2006. *Cultural Diversity and Education: Foundations, Curriculum, and Teaching.* Boston: Pearson Education, Inc., p. 15.

Barba, R. H. (1998). *Science in the Multicultural Classroom.* Boston: Allyn & Bacon.

Bartolome, L. I. (1994, Summer). "Beyond the Methods Fetish: Toward a Humanizing Pedagogy." *Harvard Educational Review* 64, no. 2, 173–94.

Barr, L. (1993). "The Next Step: Showing a Common History of Treatment for Minorities, Women and Gays in Media Content, Newsrooms, and Journalism Schools: A Proposal for Future Research and Suggestions for a Curriculum." A paper presented at the 76th annual meeting of the Association for Education in Journalism and Mass Communication (Kansas City, MO, August 11–14).

Brown v. Board of Education, 347 U.S. 483 (1954) (USSC+). Supreme Court of the United States.

Brunner, B., and E. Haney. n.d. "Civil Rights Timeline: Milestones in the Modern Civil Rights Movement." Internet resource from http://www.infoplease.com/spot/civilrightstimeline1.html.

California Newsreel. 2003. *Race: The Power of an Illusion*. A motion picture production by the Public Broadcasting Service (PBS).

Chan, S. 2010. "Applications of Andragogy in Multi-Disciplined Teaching and Learning." *Journal of Adult Education* 39 (2): 25–35.

Chandler, R. (1992). *Racing Toward 2001: The Force Shaping America's Religious Future*. Grand Rapids, MI: Zondervan Publishing House.

Chatterji, M. 2002. "Models and Methods for Examining Standards-Based Reforms and Accountability Initiatives: Have the Tools of Inquiry Answered Pressing Questions on Improving Schools?" *Review of Educational Research* 72 (3): 345–86.

Chung, R. R. 2008. "Beyond Assessment: Performance Assessments in Teacher Education." *Teacher Education Quarterly* 35 (1): 7–28.

Cochran, T., L. Antonczak, M. Guinibert, and D. Mulrennan. 2014. "Developing a Mobile Social Media Framework for Creative Pedagogies." Paper presented at the 10th International Conference on Mobile Learning, Madrid, Spain, February 28–March 2.

Cochran-Smith, M. (1997). "Knowledge, Skills, and Experiences for Teaching Culturally Diverse Learners: A Perspective for Practicing Teachers." In J. Irvine (Ed.), *Critical Knowledge for Diverse Teachers and Learners*, 27–88. Washington, DC: AACTE.

Cobb, P. (1994). "Where is the Mind? Constructivist and Sociocultural Perspectives on Mathematical Development." *Educational Researcher* 23, no. 7, 13–20.

Cohen, E. G. 1984. "Talking and Working Together: Status, Interactions, and Learning." In P. L. Peterson, L. C. Wilkerson, and M. Hallinan (Eds.), *The Social Context of Instruction: Group Organization and Group Processes*. New York: Academic Press, pp. 171–87.

Cohen, J. 2009. "Examining Fund Distribution for Title 1." The Ed Money Watch Blog. New America Foundation. Accessed August 24, 2009, from https://www.newamerica.org/education-policy/federal-education-budget-project/ed-money-watch/examining-fund-distribution-for-title-i/.

Cokley, Kevin O. 2002. "Testing Cross's Revised Racial Identity Model: An Examination of the Relationship between Racial Identity and Internalized Racialism." *Journal of Counseling Psychology* 49 (4): 476–83.

Conti, G. J. 1977. "Rebels with a Cause: Myles Horton and Paulo Friere." *Community College Review* 5 (1): 36–43.

Cooper, C. W. 2003. "The Detrimental Impact of Teacher Bias: Lessons Learned from Standpoint of African American Mothers." *Teacher Education Quarterly* 30 (2): 101–14.

Cooper, J. F., Jr. 1999. *Tenacious of Their Liberties: The Congregationalists in Colonial Massachusetts*. New York: Oxford University Press.

Cottrol, R. J., R. T. Diamone, and L. B. Ware. 2003. *Brown v. Board of Education: Caste, Culture, and the Constitution*. Kansas: University Press of Kansas.

Council of Chief State School Officers (CCSSO). 2011 (April). *Interstate Teacher Assessment and Support Consortium (InTASC) Model Core Teaching Standards: A Resource for State Dialogue.* Washington, DC: Author.

Covey, S. 1986. *The Seven Habits of Highly Effective People.* Gahanna, OH: Covey Leadership Center.

Cubberley, E. P. 1909. *Changing Conceptions of Education.* Boston: Houghton Mifflin.

Cuzzort, R. P., and E. W. King. 1976. *Humanity and Modern Social Thought.* Hindsale, IL: Dryden Press, p. 48.

The Declaration of Independence. 1776. Retrieved from http://www.ushistory.org/declaration/document.

Derman-Sparks, L. 1993. *Anti-Bias Curriculum: Tools for Empowering Young Children.* Washington, DC: Author.

Diaz-Rico, Lynne T., and Kathryn Z. Weed. 1995. *The Cross-Cultural, Language, and Academic Development Handbook: A Complete K–12 Reference Guide.* Boston: Allyn and Bacon.

Diaz-Rico, L. T., and K. Z. Weed. 2006. *The Cross-Cultural, Language, and Academic Development Handbook.* Boston: Pearson Education, Inc.

Du Bois, W. E. B. 1935. *Black Reconstruction in America.* New York: Harcourt Brace.

Durkheim, E. 1915. *The Elementary Forms of the Religious Life: A Study of Religious Sociology.* New York: Macmillan.

Edsource. 2003 (September/October). "Standards in Focus." *Leadership* 33 (1): 28–31.

Etzioni, A. 1968. *The Active Society: A Theory of Societal and Political Processes.* New York: Free Press.

Falk, B. 2002. "Standards-Based Reforms: Problems and Possibilities." *Phi Delta Kappan* 83 (8): 612–20.

Ford, N. M. 1988. *When Did I Begin? Conception of the Human Individual in History, Philosophy and Science.* New York: Cambridge University Press.

Frank, R. 2016. "Record Number of Millionaires Living in the U.S." Retrieved from http://www.cnbc.com/2016/03/07/record-number-of-millionaires-living-in-the-us.html.

Friedland, E. 2004. "Education for Liberation: Making the Classroom a Place for Thinking and Creating." *Multicultural Education* 12 (2): 2–7.

Friere, P. 1998. "Cultural Action and Conscientization." *Harvard Educational Review* 68 (4): 499–510.

Fueyo, V., and S. Bechtol. (1999, Summer). "Those Who Can, Teach: Reflecting Teaching Diverse Populations." *Teacher Education Quarterly* 26, no. 3. Retrieved from http://www.teqjournal.org/sample_issue/article_2.htm.

Gay, G. 2004. "Educational Equality for Students of Color." In *Multicultural Education: Issues and Perspectives* by J. A. Banks and C. A. McGee- Banks. New York: John Wiley and Sons.

Glenn, S. S., M. E. Malott, M. A. P. A. Andrey, M. Benvenuti, R. A. Houmanfer, I. Sandaker, J. C. Todorou, E. Z. Tourinho, and L. A. Vasconcelos. 2016. "Towards Consistent Terminology in Behaviorist Approach to Cultural Analysis." *Behavioral & Social Issues*, no. 25, 11–27.

Gollnick, D. M., and P. C. Chinn. 2009. *Multicultural Education in a Pluralistic Society*. Upper Saddle, NJ: Pearson Education.

Gorski, P. 2004. "Multicultural Pavilion." Accessed October 8, 2007 from http://www.edchange.org/multicultural.

Guggenheim, D. 2010. *Waiting for Superman* (Trailer). Retrieved from https://www.youtube.com/watch?v=ZKTfaro96dg.

Hawkins, R. P. 1990. "The Life and Contributions of Burrhus Frederick Skinner." *Education and Treatment of Children* 13 (3): 258–63.

Hernandez-Sheets, R. 2009. "What Is Diversity Pedagogy?" *Multicultural Education* 16 (3): 11–17.

Hernandez-Tutop, J. E. 1998. "Oppressor: The Educational System." Opinion Paper published by the U.S. Department of Education. Retrieved from https://eric.ed.gov/?id=ED424329.

Hertzler, J. O. 1946. *Social Institutions*. Lincoln, NE: University of Nebraska Press, p. 4.

Hildago, N. (1993). "Multicultural Teacher Introspection." In T. Perry and J. Fraser (Eds.), *Freedom's Plow: Teaching in the Multicultural Classroom*. New York: Routledge.

Internet World Stats. 2016. "Top 20 Countries with the Highest Internet Users." Retrieved from http://www.internetworldstats.com/top20.htm.

Irons, P. 2002. *Jim Crow's Children: The Broken Promise of the Brown Decision*. New York: Penguin.

Jarret, J. L. (1969). *The Educational Theorists of the Sophists*. New York: Teachers College Press.

Jones, J. M. 1997. *Prejudice and Racism*. New York: McGraw-Hill.

Kalven, J. (1982). "Personal Value Clarification." In B. Hall, J. Kalven, L. Rosen, and B. Taylor (Eds.), *Readings in Value Development*. Ramsey, NJ: Paulist Press.

Keck, S., and S. C. Kinney. 2005 (September). "Creating a Differentiated Classroom." *Learning and Leading with Technology*.

Kellog, W. O. 1995. *American History: The Easy Way*. New York: Barron's Educational Series.

Kenyon, C., and S. Hase. 2001. "Moving from Andragogy to Hetuagogy in Vocational Education." In *Research to Reality: Putting VET Research to Work*. Proceedings of the Australian Vocational Education and Training Research Association (AVETRA) conference, Adelaide, Australia, March 28–30.

Kirp, D. 1993. "The Educational Equities in Historical Perspective." In *Historical Perspectives on the Current Education Reforms*, edited by Diane Ravitch and Maris Vinovskis. Essays commissioned by the Office of Research (OR) in the Office of Educational Research and Improvement (OERI), U.S. Department of Education.

Klarman, M. J. 2004. *From Jim Crow to Civil Rights: The Supreme Court and the Struggle for Racial Equality*. New York: Oxford University Press.

Knoema. 2016. "Wealth of the World's Richest People vs. GDP of Countries." Retrieved from https://knoema.com/infographics/wqezguc/wealth-of-the-world-s-richest-people-vs-gdp-of-countries.

Koppelman, K., and R. L. Goodhart. 2005. *Understanding Human Differences: Multicultural Education for Diverse America.* Boston: Pearson Education.

Kozol, J. 1991. *Savage Inequalities: Children in America's Schools.* New York: Crown Publishers.

Kozol, J. 2005. *The Shame of the Nation: The Restoration of Apartheid Schooling in America.* New York: Crown Publishers.

Kraft, C. 1979. *Christianity in Culture.* Maryknoll, NY: Orbis Books.

Kroeber, A. L., and C. Kluckhohn, with W. Untereiner. 1952. *Culture: A Critical Review of Concepts and Definitions.* Appendices by Alfred G. Meyer. Cambridge, MA: The Museum.

Ladson-Billings, G. 1995. "But That's Just Good Teaching! The Case for Culturally Relevant Pedagogy." *Theory into Practice* 34 (3): 159–65.

La Morte, M. W. 1999. *School Law: Cases and Concepts.* Boston, MA: Allyn and Bacon.

Lasswell, T. E., J. H. Burma, and S. H. Aronson (Eds.). 1970. *Life in Society: Readings in Sociology.* Glenview, IL: Scott, Foresman and Company.

Lee, E., and R. Bhuyan. 2013. "Negotiating within Whiteness in Cross-Cultural Clinical Encounters." *Social Service Review* 87 (1): 98–130.

Levin, J., and W. Levin. 1982. *The Functions of Discrimination and Prejudice* (2nd ed.). New York: Harper & Row.

Liao, J. 2013. "The Human Body at the Intersection of Art and Science." *The Lance* 381 (9866): 525.

Library of Congress. (1995). The Gettysburg Address. Retrieved from https://www.loc.gov/exhibits/gettysburg-address/ext/trans-hay-draft.html.

Lindsay, D. (Ed.). n.d. *Abraham Lincoln/Jefferson Davis: A House Divided.* Cleveland, OH: Howard Allen.

Lindsey, R. B., L. M. Roberts, and F. Campbell-Jones. 2005. *The Culturally Proficient School: An Implementation Guide for School Leaders.* Thousand Oaks, CA: Corwin.

Lindsey, R. B., K. N. Robins, and R. D. Terrell. 1999. *Cultural Proficiency: A Manual for School Leaders.* Thousand Oaks, CA: Corwin.

MacKenzie, K. K. 2001. "Using Literacy Booster Groups to Maintain and Extend Reading Recovery Success in the Primary Grades." *The Reading Teacher* 55 (3): 222–34.

Maclay, K. 2003. "Anthropology Professor John Ogbu Dies at Age 64." Accessed October 7, 2006, from http://www.berkeley.edu/news/media/releases/2003/08/26_ogbu.shtml.

Maslow, A. 1968. *Toward a Psychology of Being.* New York: Van Nostrand Reinhold.

Mehan, H., I. Villanueva, L. Hubbard, and A. Lintz. (1996). *Constructing School Success: The Consequences of Untracking Low-Achieving Students.* New York: Cambridge University Press.

Moate, R. M., and J. A. Cox. 2015. "Learner-Centered Pedagogy: Considerations for Application in a Didactic Course." *The Professional Counselor* 5 (3): 379–89.

Montalto, N. V. 1982. *A History of the Intercultural Educational Movement, 1924–1941.* New York: Garland.

Moses, M. S., J. T. Yun, and P. Marin. 2009. "Affirmative Action's Fate: Are 20 Years More Years Enough?" *Education Policy Analysis Archives* 17 (17): 1–38.

Moses, R., and C. E. Cobb Jr. 2001. *Radical Equations: Math Literacy and Civil Rights*. Boston: Beacon Press.

Nagai, H. 2002. "Multicultural Education in the United States and Japan." Paper presented at the 46th Annual Conference of Comparative International Education Society (CIES), Orlando, Florida, March 6–8.

Nash, G. 1993. "Multiculturalism and History: Historical Perspectives and Present Prospects." In *Historical Perspectives on the Current Education Reforms*, edited by Diane Ravitch and Maris Vinovskis (Eds.). Essays commissioned by the Office of Research (OR) in the Office of Educational Research and Improvement (OERI), U.S. Department of Education.

National Center for Learning Disability, 2006. *IDEA Parent Guide*. New York: National Center for Learning Disability.

Nieto, S. 2004. *Affirming Diversity: The Sociopolitical Context of Multicultural Education*. Boston: Pearson Education.

Nieto, S., and P. Bode 2012. *Affirming Diversity: The Sociopolitical Context of Multicultural Education* (6th ed.). Boston: Pearson, pp. 110–12.

Nisbet, R. A. 1965. *Emile Durkheim*. Westport, CT: Greenwood Press.

No Child Left Behind. Available at https://www2.ed.gov/policy/elsec/leg/esea02/index.html.

Oakes, J. (1985). *Keeping Track: How Schools Structure Inequality*. New Haven, CT: Yale University Press.

Oakes, J., and M. Lipton. 1999. *Teaching to Change the World*. Boston: McGraw-Hill College.

Ozuah, P. O. 2005. "First, There Was Pedagogy and Then Came Andragogy." *Einstein Journal of Biology and Medicine* 21 (2): 83–87.

Parsons, C. V., and J. M. DeLucia. 2005 (September). "Decision Making in the Process of Differentiation." *Learning and Leading with Technology*.

Plessy v. Ferguson, 163 U.S. 537 [1896].

Pulliam, J. D., and J. J. Van Patten. 2003. *History of Education in America*. Upper Saddle River, NJ: Pearson Education.

Raths, L., M. Harmin, and S. Simon. 1966. *Values and Teaching: Working with Values in the Classroom*. Columbus, OH: Charles E. Merrill.

Reichenbach, A. 2016. "Human Skulls Found in Schuylkill County." Retrieved from http://wkok.com/human-skull-found-in-schuylkill-county/.

Romberg, T. A. (1992). "Problematic Features of the School Mathematics Curriculum." In P. N. Sackson (Ed.), *Handbook of Research on Curriculum*, 749–88. New York: MacMillan.

Romo, J. J., P. Bradfield, and R. Serrano. 2004. *Reclaiming Democracy: Multicultural Educators' Journeys toward Transformative Teaching*. Upper Saddle River, NJ: Pearson Education.

Ryan, A. 1998. "Deweyan Pragmatism and the American Education." In A. O. Rorty (Ed.), *Philosophers on Education*. New York: Routledge.

Sadkler, D., and M. Sadkler. 1994. *Teachers, Schools and Society*. Princeton, NJ: McGraw-Hill.

Salazar, L., C. A. Falkenberg, S. Nullman, M. C. Silio, and A. Nevin. 2004. "Universal Design and Differentiated Instruction: A Position Paper to Resolve Potentially Competing Mandates of the Individuals with Disabilities Education Act and No Child left Behind." Submitted to *Resources in Education*.

Schaff, P. 1888. *History of the Christian Church*. Peabody, MA: Hendrickson.

Schon, D. A. 1983. *The Reflective Practitioner: How Professionals Think in Action*. New York: Basic Books.

Secombe, M. J. 2016. "Core Values and Human Values in Intercultural Space." *Politeja*: 44, 265–75.

Sheets, R. H. 2005. *Diversity Pedagogy: Examining the Role of Culture in the Teaching-Learning Process*. Boston: Pearson Education.

Shulman, L. 1987. "Knowledge and Teaching: Foundations of the New Reform." *Harvard Educational Review* 57 (1): 1–22.

Skinner, B. F. 1968. *The Technology of Teaching*. New York: Meredith Corporation.

Sleeter, C., M. N. Torres, and P. Laughlin. 2004. "Scaffolding Conscientization through Inquiry in Teacher Education." *Teacher Education Quarterly* 31 (1): 81–96.

Smolicz, J. J. 1999. *JJ Smolicz on Education and Culture*. Margaret J. Secombe and Joseph I. Zajda, eds. Melbourne: James Nicholas Publishers.

Soukhanov, A. H. 2001. *Microsoft Encarta College Dictionary*. New York: St. Martin's.

Suleiman, M. F. 1996. "Preparing Teachers for the Culturally Diverse Classrooms." Paper presented at the 7th Annual Effective Schools Conference (Topeka, Kansas, May 3–5).

Taylor, B., and M. Kroth. 2009. "A Single Conversation with a Wise Man Is Better Than Ten Years of Study: A Model for Testing Methodologies for Pedagogy or Andragogy." *Journal of the Scholarship of Teaching and Learning* 9 (2): 42–56.

Taylor, L. S., and C. R. Whittaker. 2003. *Bridging Multiple Worlds: Case Studies of Diverse Educational Communities*. Boston: Pearson Education.

Thompson, S. 2001. "The Authentic Standards Movement and Its Evil Twin." *Phi Delta Kappan* 82 (5): 358–62.

Tiedt, P., and I. Tiedt. 2002. *Multicultural Teaching: A Handbook of Activities, Information, and Resources*. Boston: Allyn and Bacon.

Tischler, H. L., P. Whitten, and D. E. K. Hunter. 1986. *Introduction to Sociology*. New York: CBS College Publishing.

"Title VII of the Civil Rights Act of 1964." Retrieved from https://www.eeoc.gov/laws/statutes/titlevii.cfm.

Titus, H. 1970. *Living Issues in Philosophy*. New York: Cambridge University Press.

Tofler, A. 1990. *Powershift: Knowledge, Wealth, and Violence at the Edge of the 21st Century*. New York: Bantam Books.

Tomlinson, C. A. 1995. *How to Differentiate Instruction in Mixed-Ability Classrooms*. Alexandria, VA: Association for Supervision and Curriculum Development.

Tomlinson, C. A. 1999. *Differentiated Classroom: Responding to the Need of All Learners.* Alexandria, VA: Virginia Association of Supervision and Curriculum Development.

Tomlinson, C. A. 2000. *Differentiation of Instruction in the Elementary Grades."* ERIC Digest.

Ueda, R. 1993. "The Construction of Ethnic Diversity and National Identity in the Public Schools." In *Historical Perspectives on the Current Education Reforms,* edited by Diane Ravitch and Maris Vinovskis. Essays commissioned by the Office of Research (OR) in the Office of Educational Research and Improvement (OERI), U.S. Department of Education.

United States Supreme Court. (1974). *Lau v. Nichols,* No. 72-6520. Retrieved from http://supct.law.cornell.edu/supct/html/histories/USSC.

U.S. Census Bureau, U.S. Department of Justice, U.S. Office of Management and Budget. 2016. Retrieved from http://www.edchange.org/multicultural.

U.S. Supreme Court. (2017). *Brown v. Board of Education of Topeka,* 347 U.S. 483 (1954). Retrieved from https://supreme.justia.com/cases/federal/us/347/483/case.html.

U.S. Department of Education. 1993–1994. "A 1993–94 U.S. Department of Education, National Center for Educational Statistics, School Staffing Survey Reported the Percentage of Public School Teachers Who Are White, Non-Hispanic between 84 and 87 Percent." Retrieved from http://nces.ed.gov/pubs97/97460.pdf.

U.S. Department of Education. 1974. "Equal Educational Opportunities Act (EEOA)." Retrieved from http://lawhigheredu.com/52-equal-educational-opportunities-act-eeoa.html.

U.S. Equal Employment Opportunities Commission. 1964. "Title VII of the Civil Rights Act of 1964." Retrieved from https://www.eeoc.gov/laws/statutes/titlevii.cfm.

The U. S. Constitution. (2017). Retrieved from http://constitutionus.com.

Valenzuela, A. (1999). *Subtractive Schooling: U.S.-Mexican Youth and the Politics of Caring.* Albany, NY: State University of New York Press.

Wade, B. 1998. "Introduction: Literacy and Schooling." *Educational Review* 50 (2): 103–4.

Wang, J., and S. J. Odell. 2002. "Mentored Learning to Teach According to Standards-Based Reform: A Critical Review." *Review of Educational Research* 72 (3): 481–546.

Weber, M. 1958. *The Protestant Ethic and the Spirit of Capitalism.* Translated by Talcott Parsons. New York: Charles Scribner's Sons.

Weiler, J. 1998. "Recent Changes in School Desegregation." ERIC/CUE Digest Number 133.

Weinberg, D. R. 2011 (Winter). "Montessori, Maslow, and Self-Actualization." *Montessori Life,* pp. 16–21.

Weymeyer, M. L., and M. Schwartz. 2001. "Disproportionate Representation of Males in Special Education Services: Biology, Behavior, or Bias?" *Education and Treatment of Children* 24 (1): 28–45.

Williams, G. W. (1882–1883). *History of the Negro Race in America from 1619 to 1880: Negroes as Slaves, as Soldiers, and as Citizens.* New York: Putnam.

Woodson, C. G., and C. H. Wesley. 1922. *The Negro in Our History*. Washington, DC: Associated Publishers.

Yonezawa, S., A. S. Wells, and I. Serna. (2002). "Choosing Tracks: 'Freedom of Choice' in Detracking Schools." *American Educational Research Journal* 39, no. 1, 37–67.

Znaniecki, F. 1968. *The Method of Sociology*. New York: Octagon Books.

Index

abolitionist(s), 97
additive approach, 104, 117
adult learning, 2–3
African American Studies, 101
African American(s), 6, 19–20, 25–27, 59, 61, 63–64, 72–74, 77–80, 86–87, 89–91, 93–94, 97–102, 105–107, 131, 137, 140, 144
allegory of the cave, 4–6
American capitalism, 49–50
American Council on Education (ACE), 101
American family, 44
American religious landscape, 51
andragogy, 2–3, 133, 143, 146–148
Anti-defamation League (ADL), 101
Asian(s), 64, 77–79, 110; American, 28; blood, 25; countries, 43; cultural values, 28; descent, 27, 78; students, 28; studies, 101
assessment(s), 91, 116–117, 119–124, 129, 133, 142, 144
assimilation, 20, 75
assimilationist, 75

Banks, James, 83, 91, 95–96, 98, 100, 104–105, 117–118, 126–127, 131, 137, 139–143, 145

bias, 57–58, 70, 72–73, 80, 87, 137, 144, 150
biculturalism, 33, 77
Brown v. Board of Education, 99
Buddhism, 40

Civil Rights, xi, 52–54, 76, 84–85, 95, 97–100, 102, 111, 132, 138, 140–141, 143, 146–147, 149; act of 1875, 84; movement, xi, 52, 76, 95, 99–100, 111, 138, 140, 143
cluster bombs, 42
Commission on Equal Employment Opportunity, 102
Common Core State Standards (CCSS), 113, 115–116, 121–122, 125, 130
communication, 6, 20, 114, 134, 137
community, 18, 20, 22–23, 25, 40, 44, 74, 81, 86–87, 93–94, 97, 99, 106, 108–109, 114, 121–122, 124, 127, 129, 141, 144, 153
competition, 21, 39, 50, 123
Confucianism, 40
Congress of Racial Equality (CORE), 99
constitutional right, 44, 89, 102
content integration, 98
content knowledge, 121

contributions approach, 104,
Council of Chief State School Officers (CCSSO), 114, 142, 144
creativity, 26, 114, 121
critical thinking, 114, 121
cross-cultural: belief system, 70; encounters, xii, 57, 59, 61, 63, 65, 67, 71, 73–75, 77, 79, 81; harmony, 58; ideas, 68–69
Cross-cultural Language and Academic Development (CLAD), 137, 144–145
cultural characteristics, 40, 83, 96
cultural competency, xii, 63–64, 67
cultural pluralism, 77, 97, 137
cultural psyche, 64
cultural values, 28, 57–58, 60–65, 68, 86
cultural values adjustment, 57–58, 60–62, 64–65, 67–68
culture(s), xii, 3–4, 13–14, 19, 21–22, 25–29, 31–39, 42–43, 47–49, 51, 55–57, 62–66, 68, 70–77, 71, 73–79, 93, 95–96, 98, 101, 106–108, 110, 114, 117–118, 121, 123, 130, 134–135, 138, 142, 144, 146, 148; African American, 19, 26; American, 31–36, 39, 43; Korean-American, 28; Mexican, 130
curriculum content, 79, 90, 110, 115, 125
curriculum knowledge, 122

Declaration of Independence, 41, 135, 137, 144
desegregation, 98–99, 140, 149
Dewey, John, 2
differentiated instruction, 113, 119–120, 122, 142, 148
differentiation, 119–120, 123, 142, 147, 149
discrimination, vii, 17, 44, 58, 79–80, 88, 94, 100–103, 109, 111, 126–127, 131, 136, 146
diverse curricula content, 97

diversity, ix, xi, 13–14, 18–21, 27, 61, 63–64, 68, 95–97, 118, 142, 147; cultural diversity, 27, 66, 105, 130, 142–143; ethnic, 76, 106, 139, 149; pedagogy, 136, 142, 145, 148; studies, 104
dogma, 61

economic substructures, 38, 40
educational process, v, 1–5, 7, 9, 11, 17, 96
educational skill, 3
educational system(s), 6, 14, 17, 65, 71, 75, 83, 86, 89–90, 96–97, 107, 123, 139, 145
Eisenhower, Dwight, 100
elitism, 59
Elliott, Jane, 104, 108–109
empowering school culture, 98
enculturation, 5, 71, 74–75
equal education, 83–84, 87–89, 92, 99, 102–104, 141, 149
Equal Education Act of 1974, 103
equity pedagogy, 98–99, 123
ethnic, 20, 27–29, 32, 53, 62, 64–67, 70–71, 73–77, 81, 83, 90, 94, 96–98, 100, 105, 118, 123, 127; attitudes, 105; content, 118; diversity, 106, 137, 139, 149; minority(ies), 100–101; population, 101; studies, 100–101, 105, 143
ethnicity(ies), 13, 19–20, 25–26, 39, 57, 60, 72–73, 79, 94, 96, 105, 127
ethnocentric, 6, 64
etiquette(s), 35, 60, 76, 79
Eurocentric, 57, 90, 101; curriculum, 97
Every Student Succeeds Act (ESSA), 91–92

Fifteenth Amendment, 97
Fourteenth Amendment, 84, 87–88, 97, 102, 138
First Amendment, 36, 51

Index

Franklin, Benjamin, 49, 136
Freire, Paulo, 104, 107–108

gay marriage, 46, 54
gender, 13, 53, 76, 79, 83, 90, 95–96, 103, 110, 127; discrimination, 79; equality, 98; role, 105; sensitivity, 58
Gifted and Talented (GATE), 71, 91
global: age, 57; awareness, 123; battle, 36; issues, 121, 123; knowledge, 123; society, xii; trend, 33; village, xii
Global Positioning Satellites (GPS), 42

Harlem, 6
hegemony, 74
heutagogy, 3
Hinduism, 16, 40
Hispanic Studies programs, 101

individualism, 44, 50
inequality, 83, 85, 90, 93–94, 101, 106, 109
innovation, 114, 133
institutionalization, 39
instructional strategies, 110, 116, 121, 128
intercultural education, 97, 139, 147
integration, 64; content integration, 98
cultural integration, 110, 119
physical integration, 98
social integration, 61
Interstate New Teacher Assessment and Support Consortium (INTASC), 121–122, 142, 144
Islam, 16, 40, 54

Jim Crow, xi, 84, 97, 111, 138–139, 145–146
Judeo-Christian, 16; economic principles, 50; elements, 50; perspective, 16; protestant ethic, 49; values, 39–40

knowledge construction, 98, 105
knowledge of students, 123

Lau v. Nichols, 88, 103, 138, 146
leadership, 93, 122, 133, 142, 145; center, 136, 144; roles, 122; skills, 35
learner(s), v, 1–9, 11, 17–19, 21, 114, 119–122, 128, 137, 142, 149
learner-centered: classroom, 18; context, 2; curriculum, 133; education, 2; leadership, 133; pedagogy, 1, 3, 13, 18, 20, 147; practices, 133
learner development, 121
learning, vii, 2–4, 8–9, 14, 18, 21, 34, 63, 90, 104–105, 108–109, 114–116, 120–121, 123–125, 128, 133, 141–144, 146–149; activities, 1, 118–119; context, 1–2; differences, 121; disability, 147; engagement, 2; environment, 3, 18, 63, 74, 120–121; experience, 2–3, 89, 92, 121, 127; goals, 121; material(s), 2, 124; modalities, 2; objectives, 125; process, 7, 142, 148; professional learning, 122; profiles, 120; resources, 3
Luther King Jr., Martin, 35–36, 99, 109

maladjustment, 57, 63–64
male dominant, 90
Mann, Horace, 97, 139
Marshall, Thurgood, 102
Maslow, Abraham, 9, 134, 147
Meredith, James, 100
Montgomery, Alabama, 99
Montgomery Improvement Association (MIA), 99
multicultural education, i, iii, v, ix, xi–1, 3, 6, 8, 13–14, 24, 31, 57, 64, 75, 78, 83, 89–91, 95–105, 107, 109–111, 113, 115–119, 122–123, 125–126, 130–131, 135–137, 139, 141–143, 145–147
multidimensional learning, 1

National Association for the Advancement of Coloured People (NAACP), 99

National Education Association (NEA), 101
National Governors Association (NGA), 114, 121
No Child Left Behind (NCLB), 65, 91, 114, 139, 142, 147–148
North Carolina, 100

Ogbu, John, 95, 106, 141, 147
orientation to learning, 2

paidagogia, 1
Parks, Rosa, 99, 140
pedagogical, 1, 3, 124
pedagogy, 1, 121, 123, 133, 136–137, 142, 145, 147–148; culturally relevant pedagogy, 146; diversity pedagogy, 136, 142, 145, 148; equity pedagogy, 98–99, 123; in process, 108; learner-centered pedagogy, 3, 13, 18, 20, 147; of freedom, 108; of hope, 108; of the city, 108; of the heart, 108; of learning, 108; of the oppressed, 104, 108
philosophical ideologies, 40
pioneers, 97
planning, 2, 113, 119, 122, 124; instructional planning, 125; lesson planning, 124; standards-based planning, v, 113, 115, 117, 121, 123, 125; for instruction, 121
Plessey v. Ferguson, 140
pluralism, 52; cultural pluralism, 77, 97, 137
pure pluralism, 77
pluralistic, 32, 40, 51, 77; democracy, 104; ideology, 51; society, 135, 145
practice(s), i, iii, ix, xi, 33–34, 37, 40, 44, 48, 74, 79, 101, 108, 115, 120–124, 133, 137, 146; discriminatory practices, 98, 103; educational practices, 8, 44; ethical practice(s), 122; guided practice, 128; independent practice, 124, 127, 129; instructional practice(s), 119

pedagogical practice(s), 1, 3
professional practice, 65; reflective practice, 120; teaching practice(s), 121
prejudice(s), 57–60, 70–71, 79–80, 87, 98, 101, 104, 126, 136–137, 143, 145–146
prejudice reduction, 98
privilege, 61, 71, 84, 88–90, 96, 110
problem solving, 114, 120–121, 124
proficiency, 63; cultural, 63, 136, 147
progressive education, 2

racism, 23, 28, 70, 78, 80, 92, 137, 145
revisionist, 98

same sex: marriage, 46; partnerships, 53; unions, 53
San Antonio Independent School District v. Rodriguez (1973), 87, 103
school choice, 98
segregation, 84–86, 98–99, 102–103, 139
segregationists, 100
self-actualization, 8–10, 21, 134, 149
self-concept, 2, 105
self-realization, 8
separate but equal, 84–86, 89–90, 102, 138
skin pigmentation, 78
Skinner, B. F., 4, 7–8, 134, 148
social action, 66, 68, 126–127, 129–131; approach, 104, 117–118; focus, 126; objective, 113, 126, 131; project, 113, 131
social class, 83, 92, 96, 98, 107
social scientist(s), 98
social structure(s), 37–40, 44, 48, 51, 98, 107
sociologist, 38–39, 43, 95
South-Central Los Angeles, 6
Southern Christian Leadership Conference (SCLC), 99
standardization, 114, 116

standards-based instruction, 115–118, 125
Student Non-violent Coordinating Committee (SNCC), 99

teacher(s), 1, 3–4, 6–11, 14, 17, 20–24, 27, 29, 56, 58–61, 63–65, 71–74, 77–80, 88, 90–91, 93, 105, 108–110, 113, 115–130, 133, 137, 139, 141, 147–149; as accommodators, 21; as assimilators, 20; candidates, 21, 24, 72; education, ix, 21, 91, 133, 141–144, 148; educator, 71; effective, 123; expectations, 71–72; population, 91; qualified, 124; quality, 90
Teacher Performance Assessments (TPAs), 122
Title IX Education Amendment, 103
tolerance, 10, 20, 96, 117; racial, 109 religious, 40

tracking, 74, 92, 115, 122
transformation approach, 104, 118
twenty-first-century learning, 114

Ueda, Reed, 149
universal public education, 97
University of Mississippi, 100

values, 31–32, 38, 48, 58, 61–63, 75, 91, 105, 130, 136, 148; Anglo-Saxon, 75; core, 60, 148; cultural, 28, 57–58, 60–65, 67–68, 86; human, 60, 148; Judaeo-Christian, 39–40; personal, 65; social, 71

Weber, Max, 49, 136, 149
Washington, George, 35, 41
Williams, George Washington, 98

zero-sum attitudes, 59

About the Author

Chinaka S. DomNwachukwu is professor of multicultural education and associate dean for diversity and values at the School of Education, Azusa Pacific University in Azusa, California. Among his many publications are *An Introduction to Multicultural Education: From Theory to Practice* and *Multiculturalism: A Shalom Motif for the Christian Community*.

www.ingramcontent.com/pod-product-compliance
Lightning Source LLC
Chambersburg PA
CBHW030113010526
44116CB00005B/234